MacRuby: The Definitive Guide

Matt Aimonetti

O'REILLY®

Beijing · Cambridge · Farnham · Köln · Sebastopol · Tokyo

MacRuby: The Definitive Guide
by Matt Aimonetti

Copyright © 2012 Matt Aimonetti. All rights reserved.
Printed in the United States of America.

Published by O'Reilly Media, Inc., 1005 Gravenstein Highway North, Sebastopol, CA 95472.

O'Reilly books may be purchased for educational, business, or sales promotional use. Online editions are also available for most titles (*http://my.safaribooksonline.com*). For more information, contact our corporate/institutional sales department: (800) 998-9938 or *corporate@oreilly.com*.

Editors: Mike Loukides and Andy Oram	**Indexer:** Jay Marchand
Production Editor: Adam Zaremba	**Cover Designer:** Karen Montgomery
Copyeditor: Amy Thomson	**Interior Designer:** David Futato
Proofreader: Teresa Horton	**Illustrator:** Robert Romano

October 2011:   First Edition.

Revision History for the First Edition:
    2011-10-12   First release
See *http://oreilly.com/catalog/errata.csp?isbn=9781449380373* for release details.

ISBN: 978-1-449-38037-3

[LSI]

1318437555

Pour ma fille, Giana,

Et pour ma femme, Heidi: merci pour ton soutien, tes encouragements, et ta compréhension. Sans toi, ce livre n'aurait jamais vu le jour.

Table of Contents

Preface

MacRuby is Apple's implementation of the Ruby programming language on top of the Objective-C technology stack. It allows developers to write native applications for the Cocoa environment using the popular Ruby syntax as well as the well-known and robust Objective-C and C libraries.

This book provides a guide to OS X development for MacRuby developers. Key concepts of MacRuby and Cocoa, as well the popular Cocoa APIs, are covered in this book. The book should help you leverage your existing programming knowledge to make you an efficient and productive MacRuby developer.

I became interested in MacRuby after many years working on/with/around Ruby web frameworks. I started using MacRuby after meeting Laurent Sansonetti (MacRuby lead developer at Apple). Laurent showed me that MacRuby had some interesting things to offer: a programming language that I liked as well as some great APIs and tools that allowed me to develop desktop applications easily and access some cool hardware resources.

This book was written using a version of MacRuby just prior 1.0. All the Xcode screenshots were created using Xcode 4.x. Most, if not all, of the content should be valid for MacRuby 1.x. and later versions.

The Purpose of This Book

The purpose of this book is to:

- Teach MacRuby fundamentals.
- Provide a guide to develop Cocoa applications using the MacRuby language.
- Show concrete examples leveraging the Cocoa technology using MacRuby.

My personal goal is to provide you with a solid foundation, allowing you to understand how MacRuby is meant to be used and why things are designed the way they are. While this book is neither a Ruby book nor a Cocoa book, it should provide you with enough information to understand the MacRuby environment and create rich applications for the OS X platform.

Prerequisites

To get the most out of this book, you should have some programming experience and be familiar with the basics of object-oriented programming. I also assume some very basic knowledge of Ruby, because there are so many places to pick up that knowledge and the language is pretty simple. If you aren't familiar with Ruby yet, go to the Ruby language website (*http://www.ruby-lang.org*) and read up. You'll get more out of this book if you do that first. If you are already familiar with Ruby but would like to learn more, I recommend the excellent book, *The Ruby Programming Language* (*http://amzn .to/prog-ruby*), by David Flanagan and Ruby's creator, Yukihiro Matsumoto.

Also, even though we are going to cover some of the basics, understanding some fundamental Cocoa concepts will help. You can learn more about Cocoa as you go along, but should you find something confusing in this book, here are places to look for more information:

- Apple's dev center (*http://developer.apple.com*)
- Your local CocoaHeads group (*http://cocoaheads.org*)
- One of the many available books, such as:
  - Aaron Hillegass's books (Aaron wrote a Cocoa programming book [*http:// bignerdranch.com/book/cocoa%C2%AE_programming_for_mac%C2%AE_os _x_3rd_edition*] and an advanced Mac OS X programming [*http://bignerdranch .com/book/advanced_mac_os_x_programming_nd_edition_*] book.)
  - Cocoa Programming: A Quick-Start Guide for Developers (*http://pragprog.com/ titles/dscpq/cocoa-programming*)

Conventions Used in This Book

The following typographical conventions are used in this book:

Italic
> Indicates new terms, URLs, email addresses, filenames, and file extensions.

`Constant width`
> Used for program listings, as well as within paragraphs to refer to program elements such as variable or function names, databases, data types, environment variables, statements, and keywords.

`Constant width bold`
> Shows commands or other text that should be typed literally by the user.

`Constant width italic`
> Shows text that should be replaced with user-supplied values or by values determined by context.

This icon signifies a tip, suggestion, or general note.

 This icon indicates a warning or caution.

Using Code Examples

This book is here to help you get your job done. In general, you may use the code in this book in your programs and documentation. You do not need to contact us for permission unless you're reproducing a significant portion of the code. For example, writing a program that uses several chunks of code from this book does not require permission. Selling or distributing a CD-ROM of examples from O'Reilly books does require permission. Answering a question by citing this book and quoting example code does not require permission. Incorporating a significant amount of example code from this book into your product's documentation does require permission.

We appreciate, but do not require, attribution. An attribution usually includes the title, author, publisher, and ISBN. For example: "*MacRuby: The Definitive Guide* by Matt Aimonetti (O'Reilly). Copyright 2012 Matt Aimonetti, 978-1-449-38037-3."

If you feel your use of code examples falls outside fair use or the permission given above, feel free to contact us at *permissions@oreilly.com*.

Safari® Books Online

 Safari Books Online is an on-demand digital library that lets you easily search over 7,500 technology and creative reference books and videos to find the answers you need quickly.

With a subscription, you can read any page and watch any video from our library online. Read books on your cell phone and mobile devices. Access new titles before they are available for print, and get exclusive access to manuscripts in development and post feedback for the authors. Copy and paste code samples, organize your favorites, download chapters, bookmark key sections, create notes, print out pages, and benefit from tons of other time-saving features.

O'Reilly Media has uploaded this book to the Safari Books Online service. To have full digital access to this book and others on similar topics from O'Reilly and other publishers, sign up for free at *http://my.safaribooksonline.com*.

How to Contact Us

Please address comments and questions concerning this book to the publisher:

O'Reilly Media, Inc.
1005 Gravenstein Highway North
Sebastopol, CA 95472
800-998-9938 (in the United States or Canada)
707-829-0515 (international or local)
707-829-0104 (fax)

We have a web page for this book, where we list errata, examples, and any additional information. You can access this page at:

http://shop.oreilly.com/product/0636920000723.do

To comment or ask technical questions about this book, send email to:

bookquestions@oreilly.com

For more information about our books, courses, conferences, and news, see our website at *http://www.oreilly.com.*

Find us on Facebook: *http://facebook.com/oreilly*

Follow us on Twitter: *http://twitter.com/oreillymedia*

Watch us on YouTube: *http://www.youtube.com/oreillymedia*

Acknowledgments

I would like to start out by thanking the two people without whom MacRuby would have never existed:

- Yukihiro Matsumoto (Matz), for designing Ruby, such an elegant language.
- Laurent Sansonetti, for writing the MacRuby implementation and leading the project.

I'm grateful to Apple for initiating and supporting the MacRuby project (with special thanks to Jordan Hubbard), and to Steve Jobs, who through his life proved that passionate people casting a vision of simplicity, efficiency, and interaction can design products that change the world. In addition, I'd like to thank my MacRuby teammates: Laurent Sansonetti, Vincent Isambart, Eloy Duran, Thibault Martin-Lagardette, Satoshi Nakagawa, Joshua Ballanco, Watson, Takao Kouji, Rich Kilmer, Patrick Thomson, and all the many contributors to the project over the years.

I would also like to thank J. Chris Anderson and Jan Lehnardt, who inspired me to release my work under the Creative Commons Attribution license, with a special "thank you" to Jan for introducing me to Mike Loukides. Speaking of Mike, I'd like to thank him and Andy Oram from O'Reilly for assisting and encouraging me as I wrote this book. Next, I'd like to thank the dozens of reviewers who gave me insightful comments and suggestions. You are too many to be listed, but know that I really appreciate you taking the time to help me make this book better.

Finally, I'd like to thank my friends and family for their continuous support and encouragement.

MacRuby Overview

Part I introduces MacRuby. What is it? How do you install it? How does it work? What can you do with it? How does it relate to what you already know? These are the sorts of questions answered here.

## CHAPTER 1

Introduction

If you are interested in developing applications for Apple's Mac OS X platform, you probably know that it's intimately tied in with the Objective-C language. Objective-C extends the standard ANSI C language by adding full object-oriented programming capabilities. It sees little use outside Apple environments.

Objective-C presents quite a contrast to Ruby, a scripting language that became very popular, thanks in part to the Ruby on Rails web framework. Both languages are very dynamic (although Objective-C is fully compiled) and object-oriented. They both have comparable levels of introspection, support metaprogramming, and have their own garbage collector. But Objective-C is a verbose language with rather tiresome requirements for specifying data and methods, and it might not fit all developers. Ruby, in contrast, is sleek and encourages quick programming techniques such as prototyping. According to its creator, Yukihiro Matsumoto, Ruby is designed for humans, not machines because "We are the masters. They are the slaves." Both languages have their pros and cons. To find out more about Matsumoto, see the Wikipedia entry for Yukihiro Matsumoto (*http://en.wikipedia.org/wiki/Yukihiro_Matsumoto*).

Mac OS X ships with a version of Ruby you can access from the command line, but MacRuby is a completely separate project that has one key advantage: it provides access to all the features available to Objective-C programmers.

Introducing MacRuby

MacRuby is Apple's implementation of the Ruby programming language. More precisely, it is a Ruby implementation that invokes methods from the well-known and proven Objective-C runtime to give you direct native access to all the OS X libraries. The end result is a first-class, compilable scripting language designed to develop applications for the OS X platform.

MacRuby brings you the best of both worlds:

- The power and flexibility of Ruby
- The rock-solidness of the Objective-C runtime with the richness of the Cocoa environment

As you can see in Figure 1-1, MacRuby runs natively in the Objective-C runtime and offers Ruby as an alternative native runtime language with support for its well-known ecosystem of libraries and tools.

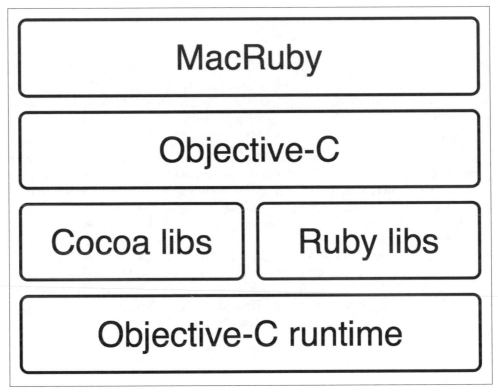

Figure 1-1. The MacRuby stack

Why MacRuby?

MacRuby has some obvious and not so obvious advantages. It is Apple's first alternate language for accessing the Objective-C runtime. What's even more interesting is that Apple managed to do this without reinventing the wheel. Instead, MacRuby is really the result of the blend of great existing technologies.

For most beginners, MacRuby's learning curve is not as steep as if you start directly with Objective-C and Cocoa. Certainly, MacRuby developers also have to learn Cocoa's APIs. However, beginners have an easier time thanks to simple things such as not having to worry about header files and implementation files, the use of a succinct and natural syntax, and the availability of an interactive shell.

A lot of documentation is available for MacRuby, although you have to learn how to interpret it because much of it assumes an Objective-C environment. In addition to MacRuby-specific documentation, such as this book, you can find a lot of documentation regarding Ruby and Cocoa. Tools used by both communities are available to MacRuby developers and you can rely on the communities to help you with domain-specific challenges.

MacRuby's open source status might not be an obvious advantage at first, but it offers direct access to the core of the implementation. The quality of the code can be easily evaluated, patches can be submitted, and overall it is a sign that Apple wants greater involvement from the developers targeting its platform, as well as offering some transparency into its technology.

MacRuby is for you if:

- You prefer to avoid C-like syntax and low-level coding.
- You are interested in learning or already know Objective-C, Ruby, Python, Perl, or Smalltalk.
- You are interested in targeting the OS X platform.

MacRuby is also for you if you are already a Cocoa developer but would like to improve your productivity, interact a bit more with the world outside of Cocoa, or maybe just improve your test coverage.

Objective-C is a great language, but it is also very verbose. The problem is not the amount of time you spend writing code (most integrated development environments [IDEs] will generate code for you anyway). The real problem is the amount of time developers spend reading and understanding the code previously written. Most of the time spent fixing a bug is not really spent "fixing" anything, but finding the source of the bug. By offering a syntax that is less verbose and easier to grasp, MacRuby instantly improves your short-term and long-term productivity.

Cocoa developers can leverage their acquired knowledge and existing code and maximize their efficiency by using MacRuby. Because Ruby, Objective-C, and C code can be used in the same project, your legacy code is 100% reusable. Available libraries for Cocoa, Ruby, and even C can help enrich your projects and save you precious time.

MacRuby has full native support for regular expressions, which might be enough to convince you to try it.

Finally, Apple's backing is recognition that a higher-level language, designed to be easy to read and enjoyable to work with while still being fully natively Cocoa compliant, is valuable to developers targeting the Apple platform.

Installation

No doubt you are impatient to start writing applications. But before we can start writing any code, we need to make sure we have all the required tools set up properly. Getting started is really simple and doesn't require compiling anything.

Mac OS X

First, make sure you are running Snow Leopard, Lion, or a more recent version of MacOS X. MacRuby runs on Leopard, but for the purpose of this book, I'll assume you are using a more recent version of the OS.

Xcode

Xcode is Apple's development environment for OS X. Installing Xcode will provide you with the tools and libraries required to develop Cocoa applications.

You can either install Xcode from the OS X DVD that shipped with your Mac or download it from Apple's developer center (*http://developer.apple.com*).

 Apple regularly updates Xcode, which means that the online version is likely more recent than the one you have on your OS X installation DVD. At the time of this writing, Apple still provides Xcode 3 for free, but Xcode 4 is sold for five American dollars at the App Store, or free if you have an iOS or Mac developer license. This book will refer to Xcode 4, but the same concepts apply to Xcode 3.

MacRuby

As of the writing of this chapter, MacRuby is not shipping with OS X or Xcode. Lion ships with MacRuby as a private framework because the OS relies on it, but because Apple didn't make the framework public, you are not allowed to link against it. So, you need to install MacRuby manually.

Installing MacRuby is easy:

1. Go to the MacRuby website (*http://macruby.org*).
2. Download the package installer.
3. Launch it to install MacRuby on your machine.

MacRuby won't conflict with the Ruby version you already have installed.

If you already have Xcode 3 installed and upgrade to Xcode 4, you will need to reinstall MacRuby so the updated version of Xcode can make proper use of the MacRuby tools.

MacRuby does not come with an uninstaller. If you want to remove MacRuby from your computer, delete the MacRuby binary files, which use the *mac* prefix and are located in */usr/local/bin/*. Then remove MacRuby itself: */Library/Frameworks/MacRuby.framework*.

MacRuby is a library/framework and end users don't need to have it installed on their machines to use your program. You can package MacRuby within your app during the building process.

Code Example

Instead of making you wade through MacRuby's history, the technical aspects of the implementations, and their pros and cons, let's dive into a code example to get a feel for MacRuby.

We'll build a traditional "Hello World!" example. To keep things simple, we'll just write a script and won't use any IDEs or GUI tools. Let's make it pretty and create a window with a button. When the button is clicked, the computer will greet the world through its speakers:

```
framework 'AppKit'
class AppDelegate
  def applicationDidFinishLaunching(notification)
    voice_type = "com.apple.speech.synthesis.voice.GoodNews"
    @voice = NSSpeechSynthesizer.alloc.initWithVoice(voice_type)
  end

  def windowWillClose(notification)
    puts "Bye!"
    exit
  end

  def say_hello(sender)
    @voice.startSpeakingString("Hello World!")
    puts "Hello World!"
  end
end

app = NSApplication.sharedApplication
app.delegate = AppDelegate.new

window = NSWindow.alloc.initWithContentRect([200, 300, 300, 100],
    styleMask:NSTitledWindowMask|NSClosableWindowMask|NSMiniaturizableWindowMask,
    backing:NSBackingStoreBuffered,
```

```
        defer:false)
  window.title       = 'MacRuby: The Definitive Guide'
  window.level       = NSModalPanelWindowLevel
  window.delegate    = app.delegate

  button = NSButton.alloc.initWithFrame([80, 10, 120, 80])
  button.bezelStyle = 4
  button.title       = 'Hello World!'
  button.target      = app.delegate
  button.action      = 'say_hello:'

  window.contentView.addSubview(button)

  window.display
  window.orderFrontRegardless
  app.run
```

Type in the code (don't worry about matching my spacing) or download it from *http://bit.ly/macruby_hello_world*, then save it in a file named *hello_world.rb* and run it in a terminal:

```
$ macruby hello_world.rb
```

The application, shown in Figure 1-2, will open.

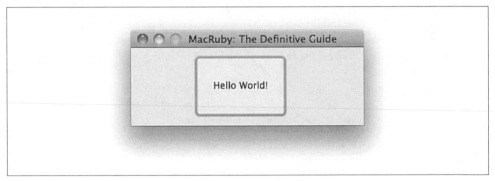

Figure 1-2. "Hello World!" example run from the command line

Congratulations, we just wrote a graphical user interface (GUI) application in 35 lines of code! And don't forget to click the button to hear your computer's nice voice.

Let's do a first walk through the code so you have a general understanding of what we just wrote.

We start by loading the `AppKit` framework, which gives us access to classes to build a GUI app. Then we create a class called `AppDelegate`, which implements methods to handle the actions our application triggers. This new class has three different methods: one to be called when the application is loaded (`applicationDidFinishLaunching`), one when the window is closed (`windowWillClose`), and one to say, "Hello world!" (`say_hello`).

After the application is launched, we create an instance of the NSSpeechSynthesizer class that we keep in an instance variable called @voice. The instance variable makes the features available to every method in the AppDelegate class. When the button is clicked, we trigger the say_hello method, which will use the voice object to greet the world. The say_hello method also outputs a string to our terminal. Finally, when the window is closed, our code says, "Bye!" and exits.

The class AppDelegate is used to create a *delegate* that is attached to another object to handle events sent to that object. Delegates have to be set for each object you want to handle events for.

To keep things simple, our delegate instance is used by all the objects in the user interface: the application, the window, and the button. So, our next step is to get a pointer to our application and link it to a new instance of our delegate class:

```
app = NSApplication.sharedApplication
app.delegate = AppDelegate.new
```

That's pretty easy, but we are not done yet. We also need to build a window with a button inside. Furthermore, assigning an application delegate to our application does not make the other objects within the application *use* the delegate. Each object has to be attached explicitly. Interface Builder offers a really nice interface that allows you to graphically define targets, making the delegate concept much easier to work with.

A window is created by passing a frame reference and a style. You can see a slight increase in the code's complexity, because we have to tell the Objective-C runtime a bunch of information.

The frame refers to the coordinate space (in points) of the window. Objective-C developers usually pass an NSRect instance. MacRuby developers can simply pass an Array with the frame references in the following order: x, y, width, height. These work like just about every other windowing system: x and y specify the position of the top left corner of the window from the top left corner of the screen, while width and height specify the window's size. The coordinates and positioning are discussed in Chapter 5:

```
window = NSWindow.alloc.initWithContentRect([200, 300, 300, 100],
    styleMask:NSTitledWindowMask|NSClosableWindowMask|NSMiniaturizableWindowMask,
    backing:NSBackingStoreBuffered,
    defer:false)
```

We also give a title to our window, set its level and style, and connect it to the delegate we previously created. The level determines how the window will stack in relation to other windows/applications. If you don't explicitly set the window level in your script, the new window will display behind the command line, which is in focus. That's why we need to set it as a modal window level—so it shows above the running application.

Now it's time to create a button, the same way we created a window. We create our button by passing a frame reference:

```
button = NSButton.alloc.initWithFrame([80, 10, 120, 80])
```

The button is styled to make it look better, give it a title, and connect it to our delegate:

```
button.target = app.delegate
```

But before moving on, we need to tell the button what to do when it's clicked, which we do by defining its action:

```
button.action = 'say_hello:'
```

Remember the say_hello method we created in our delegate? Now, when the button is clicked, the method is triggered.

 Did you notice the colon at the end of the string? It's present because we are referring to the method we want to invoke. Technically, this is called a *selector* and our selector takes an argument (the sender), so it is represented with a colon. We will discuss selectors a bit more later in this chapter, but in this case we just need to append a colon to the name of the method to make it a selector.

Once the button is created and set up, we can add it to the window:

```
window.contentView.addSubview(button)
```

Our GUI is now ready. We just need to display the window, put it on foreground, and run our application:

```
window.display
window.orderFrontRegardless
app.run
```

That was not too hard, was it?

Now start your application from the terminal:

```
$ macruby hello_world.rb
```

You'll see the application window shown in Figure 1-2.

 When executing a script via the terminal, your application won't properly get focus and you might notice some issues with text fields, for instance. To force the focus, you can use the following code:

```
NSApplication.sharedApplication.activationPolicy =
NSApplicationActivationPolicyRegular
NSApplication.sharedApplication.activateIgnoringOtherApps(true)
```

Here is more good news: using Xcode and Interface Builder, we will be able to do the same thing with even less code. But before playing with the GUI tools, let's learn more about MacRuby and Cocoa by going through the code in detail.

Loading a Framework

Our example starts with a framework:

```
framework 'AppKit'
```

A framework is a library (usually a dynamically linked library) packaged with the supporting files that make it easier for a developer to use that library. Mac OS X ships with many frameworks, and a lot of third-party frameworks are also available. In Chapter 2, you'll learn more about the Cocoa environment and some of the most commonly used frameworks.

But for now, what's important to understand is that we are loading an Objective-C framework called AppKit, also known as the *Cocoa Application Framework*. The App Kit framework provides the functionality to build OS X GUI applications. We are going to explore this framework at length in Chapter 5, so let's just focus on the rest of the code for now.

Using Classes

MacRuby is a true object-oriented language, in which everything is an object, and objects are defined by classes.

Defining a Class and Its Methods

Defining a class in MacRuby is straightforward. Use the class keyword, followed by the capitalized name of the class. To close the class definition, use the end keyword. Unlike Objective-C, no headers are required; just define your class once and you are ready to go.

Here is our AppDelegate class. As you can see, each method begins with def and ends (like the class definition) with end. I've used indentation to show how the end statements line up with the beginnings of the definitions:

```
class AppDelegate
  def applicationDidFinishLaunching(notification)
    voice_type = "com.apple.speech.synthesis.voice.GoodNews"
    @voice = NSSpeechSynthesizer.alloc.initWithVoice(voice_type)
  end

  def windowWillClose(notification)
    puts "Bye!"
    exit
  end
```

```
    def say_hello(sender)
      @voice.startSpeakingString("Hello World!")
      puts "Hello World!"
    end
  end
```

Ruby objects are initialized using the new class method. This is exactly what we did in our "Hello World!" example when we created an instance of our AppDelegate class:

```
AppDelegate.new
```

And if you look further, we have another object instantiation, this time using different methods:

```
button = NSButton.alloc.initWithFrame([80, 10, 120, 80])
```

The combination of alloc and an init method is used because NSButton is an Objective-C class and has its own constructor. To keep it simple, when dealing with classes you created or other Ruby classes, use the new constructor method. Otherwise, use alloc.init or any other constructors mentioned in the documentation (in this case, alloc.initWithFrame).

 Although you can use new to instantiate an Objective-C class, I strongly recommend you use alloc.init or related constructors defined by the class. Apple's Objective-C classes are usually easy to identify, because their names start by NS. The reason for this advice is that the class was written and tested to be used the Objective-C way and it's therefore safer to initialize it that way.

Ruby Class Instantiation

You can customize instantiation by defining the initialize method. Unlike Objective-C, Ruby doesn't have a public explicit object allocation method, but both languages initialize instances of objects immediately after they are created. Ruby has an internal allocate method but is called automatically. Ruby implicitly calls the initialize method, while Objective-C makes initialization explicit with a call to some method whose name usually begins with init.

The following example causes an instance variable in the Book class to be initialized whenever an object of that class is created with new:

```
class Book
  def initialize
    @created_at = Time.now
  end
end
```

To modify the construction of any new instances, we just reopen the class and define initialize.

By reopening the class, I mean that we define a class that was previously defined. All we do here is overwrite the `initialize` method. Classes are never closed. Both MacRuby and Objective-C classes can be reopened at any time, so it's incredibly easy to add new methods to existing classes at runtime.

Right after a new Book instance is created, a new instance variable called *@created_at* will be defined and will hold the creation time. This `@created_at` instance variable is then stored inside our newly created object.

Let's look next at how MacRuby handles methods.

Methods

Objects respond to methods. In Objective-C terminology, the invocation of a method is also called sending the object a *message*. Like variables, methods can be class methods, which are called on the name of the class, or instance methods, which are called on objects after they are created with `new`. A simple example of a class method is:

```
class Contact
  def self.first
    # Let's pretend we have an array of contacts
    # held in the @contacts class instance variable.
    @contacts.first
  end
end

Contact.first   # => #<Contact:0x20029fe20>
```

A simple instance method is:

```
class Contact
  def full_name
    "#{first_name} #{last_name}"
  end
end

Contact.first.full_name   # => "Laurent Sansonetti"
```

 Ruby methods don't need to explicitly return a value. If a method doesn't explicitly issue a return statement, the last value evaluated in the body of the method will be returned.

There can also be singleton methods. These are methods defined on an individual instance of an object, as in the following example:

```
laurent = Contact.first
def laurent.country_of_origin
  "Belgium"
```

```
end

laurent.country_of_origin # => "Belgium"
```

In this example, only the object named `laurent` can invoke the `country_of_origin` method. Singleton methods are very useful in MacRuby, because they allow you to overwrite or define a method on an instance instead of having to create a subclass.

 MacRuby methods can also be defined in many other ways, described in the Ruby language reference.

Looking at the `AppDelegate` class we created, we can see the three defined methods:

```
def applicationDidFinishLaunching(notification)
  ...
end

def windowWillClose(notification)
  ...
end

def say_hello(sender)
  ...
end
```

If you look closely at the names of the methods, you will notice that the first two are CamelCased , while the last one uses an underscore. By convention, Rubyists usually underscore their method names. But in this case, the two first methods are callbacks sent by the application. These callbacks are defined in Objective-C, so their names use the CamelCase syntax convention that's ubiquitous in Objective-C. The last method is the method we trigger when the button is pressed. We have full control over this method and we could have defined the button's action method `sayHello` to stay consistent. But instead, by using the Ruby convention, we can quickly see which methods come from Cocoa libraries and which ones we wrote. Another way to explain the same thing is that the `windowWillClose` and `applicationDidFinishLaunching` methods are predefined and can be included in our class to provide certain functionality even though we are not calling them explicitly. In comparison, `say_hello` is our own method that we call explicitly in our code and thus we can name it anything we want.

If defined on an application delegate, the `applicationDidFinishLaunching` method is triggered when the application is launched. We are using this callback to create an instance of `NSSpeechSynthesizer` that we will hold in the `@voice` instance variable:

```
def applicationDidFinishLaunching(notification)
  voice_type = "com.apple.speech.synthesis.voice.GoodNews"
  @voice = NSSpeechSynthesizer.alloc.initWithVoice(voice_type)
end
```

To find out which constructor to use to create a speech synthesizer and which voices are available, read the documentation. Apple documentation follows its own set of conventions, which I'll introduce you to next.

Documentation

When you load a framework, you get access to its APIs, which include classes, methods, constants, functions, enumerations, and so on. As I explained earlier, many frameworks are written in Objective-C. Their conventions reflect Objective-C practices, and that comes out in the documentation, which is fairly easy for Objective-C programmers to read, but could use some interpretation for other readers.

To learn more about each framework and see its possibilities, open the developer documentation and look for the framework, or search for a specific class. The documentation is available via Xcode or on Apple's developer website (*http://developer.apple .com/mac*), and it looks the same in both places.

Let's open the `NSSpeechSynthesizer` class documentation so we can see the available methods. Search for `NSSpeechSynthesizer` in the documentation and you should find the `NSSpeechSynthesizer` class reference. Under the "tasks" section, there is an entry titled "Creating Speech Synthesizers" with its first documented method called `init WithVoice`:

---

*initWithVoice:

Initializes the receiver with a voice.

    `- (id)initWithVoice:(NSString *)voiceIdentifier`

Parameters

    `voiceIdentifier`

Identifier of the voice to set as the current voice. When nil, the default voice is used. Passing in a specific voice means the initial speaking rate is determined by the synthesizer's default speaking rate; passing nil means the speaking rate is automatically set to the rate the user specifies in Speech preferences.

Return Value

Initialized speech synthesizer or nil when the voice identified by `voiceIdentifier` is not available or when there's an allocation error.

- Available in Mac OS X v10.3 and later.

See Also

    `+ availableVoices`

Declared In

    `NSSpeechSynthesizer.h`

Method prototypes

The Objective-C method signature might seem a bit cryptic at first, so let me explain what it means:

```
- (id)initWithVoice:(NSString *)voiceIdentifier
```

Notice first that the signature starts with a - symbol, which means that we are dealing with an instance method. A class method signature would start with a + symbol.

The instance method is called `initWithVoice` and returns an object of type `id`. In Objective-C, the `id` keyword means that the returned object can be of any type. In this case, the documentation explains that the returned value can be either a speech synthesizer instance or nil. Finally, the method takes an argument representing the `voiceIdentifier` to use. The argument should be a `String`. However, the documentation indicates that `nil` can also be passed.

Constant names

The documentation might refer to some constants that are relevant to the class. In Cocoa, constants are namespaced and start with a k followed by a two-letter code. For instance, AB stands for `AddressBook`, and its documentation mentions the `kABFirstNameProperty` constant. However, even though a constant can start with a lowercase character in Objective-C, in MacRuby, constants always have to start with an uppercase character. In this example, Objective-C's `kABFirstNameProperty` constant is available as `KABFirstNameProperty` in MacRuby.

The Interactive Ruby Shell

A great advantage of using MacRuby is that we can use the interactive shell to inspect our code. Let's experiment with the `NSSpeechSynthesizer` class and learn more about it by interacting directly with it.

The `NSSpeechSynthesizer` documentation sample we looked at earlier mentions a class method named + `availableVoices`. Let's play with it.

Open a terminal shell and launch *macirb* (*macirb* is MacRuby's interactive shell and it is installed when you install MacRuby):

```
$ macirb --simple-prompt
>> framework 'AppKit'
=> true
>> NSSpeechSynthesizer.availableVoices
=> ["com.apple.speech.synthesis.voice.Agnes",
"com.apple.speech.synthesis.voice.Albert",
"com.apple.speech.synthesis.voice.Alex",
"com.apple.speech.synthesis.voice.BadNews",
"com.apple.speech.synthesis.voice.Bahh",
"com.apple.speech.synthesis.voice.Bells",
"com.apple.speech.synthesis.voice.Boing",
"com.apple.speech.synthesis.voice.Bruce",
```

```
 "com.apple.speech.synthesis.voice.Bubbles",
 "com.apple.speech.synthesis.voice.Cellos",
 "com.apple.speech.synthesis.voice.Deranged",
 "com.apple.speech.synthesis.voice.Fred",
 "com.apple.speech.synthesis.voice.GoodNews",
 "com.apple.speech.synthesis.voice.Hysterical",
 "com.apple.speech.synthesis.voice.Junior",
 "com.apple.speech.synthesis.voice.Kathy",
 "com.apple.speech.synthesis.voice.Organ",
 "com.apple.speech.synthesis.voice.Princess",
 "com.apple.speech.synthesis.voice.Ralph",
 "com.apple.speech.synthesis.voice.Trinoids",
 "com.apple.speech.synthesis.voice.Vicki",
 "com.apple.speech.synthesis.voice.Victoria",
 "com.apple.speech.synthesis.voice.Whisper",
 "com.apple.speech.synthesis.voice.Zarvox"]
```

In irb mode, the chevrons (>>) represent the irb prompt, the fat arrow (⇒) represents output, and anything after a hash (#) is a comment I added.

We started macirb with the `--simple-prompt` argument to avoid displaying the line numbers. Check on the various options by passing the `--help` argument.

Let's create an instance of the speech synthesizer, passing `nil` to use the default voice, and let's see what methods are available:

```
>> voice = NSSpeechSynthesizer.alloc.initWithVoice(nil)
=> #<NSSpeechSynthesizer:0x2004c7c20>
>> voice.methods   returns the available Ruby methods
The list is too long for this book but give it a try on your machine.
>> voice.methods(true, true)   returns the available Objective-C methods
=> the list is too long for this book
>> voice.methods(true, true).grep(/speak/i)
returns all methods containing 'speak' in their name.
Limited selection for the purpose of this book.
=> [:continueSpeaking, :stopSpeaking, :isSpeaking, :startSpeakingString]
```

We created a speech synthesizer instance, inspected the Ruby and Objective-C methods, and even filtered them to find the methods used to speak.

We can invoke another method to see the status of the object, then define a string and feed it to the synthesizer to read out loud:

```
>> voice.isSpeaking
=> false
# MacRuby offers an alias to Objective-C methods starting by is
>> voice.speaking?
=> false
>> voice.respond_to?(:sing)
=> false
>> jelly_time = "Do the peanut butter jelly, peanut butter jelly,
Peanut butter jelly with a baseball bat"
```

```
=> "Do the peanut butter jelly, peanut butter jelly,
\nPeanut butter jelly with a baseball bat"
>> voice.startSpeakingString(jelly_time)
=> true
```

Now let's play with some of the other available voices we listed earlier when we called the `availableVoices` class method:

```
>> voice_name = "com.apple.speech.synthesis.voice.BadNews"
=> "com.apple.speech.synthesis.voice.BadNews"
>> voice = NSSpeechSynthesizer.alloc.initWithVoice(voice_name)
=> #<NSSpeechSynthesizer:0x200855380>
>> voice.startSpeakingString(jelly_time)
=> true
```
let's try with a different voice
```
>> voice_name = "com.apple.speech.synthesis.voice.GoodNews"
=> "com.apple.speech.synthesis.voice.GoodNews"
>> voice = NSSpeechSynthesizer.alloc.initWithVoice(voice_name)
=> #<NSSpeechSynthesizer:0x200873100>
>> voice.startSpeakingString(jelly_time)
=> true
```

Have fun trying different voices with different sentences and get a feel for *macirb*.

Syntactic Sugar

MacRuby offers a couple of method aliases to keep your code more Ruby-like. Feel free to use whichever version you prefer:

Objective-C/Ruby accessor syntax:

```
object.setFoo(bar)
object.foo = bar
```

Objective-C/Ruby boolean response syntax:

```
object.isFoo
object.foo?
```

Objective-C/Ruby key accessor syntax:

```
keyed_object.objectForKey('foo')
keyed_object['foo']
```

Objective-C/Ruby key setter:

```
keyed_object.setObject('bar', :forKey => 'foo')
keyed_object['foo'] = bar
```

The Ruby syntax is usually shorter than the Objective-C syntax, but it is good to know both for times when you go back and forth between Objective-C and Ruby code.

Some extra helpers added by MacRuby include:

Convert a String *instance into an* NSData:

```
"this is a test".to_data
```

Convert an NSData *instance into a* String:

```
data = "this is a test".to_data
# => #<NSCFData:0x200245d40>
data.to_str
# => "this is a test"
```

Convert an object into a property list:

```
[1, "two", {'three' => 3}, true, false].to_plist
```

Load and convert a property list:

```
plist = {one: 1, two: 2, three: 3}.to_plist
load_plist(plist)
```

## CHAPTER 2

Fundamentals

This chapter focuses on the fundamentals of GUI application development. It covers the concepts of run loops, callbacks and delegation, user inputs, outlets, and display. Finally, these basic concepts are illustrated in an example application.

Figure 2-1 shows the simplified view that most users have when it comes to applications.

Figure 2-1. The way my mom sees herself using one of my applications

If we give it a closer look, we will notice some key elements my mom takes for granted. My mom has a good perspective that we don't need to disagree with. From her perspective, she is simply having an interaction with her computer. She opens the application, clicks, types, and sees a result right away. However, what's going on under the covers is a bit more complex, as shown in Figure 2-2.

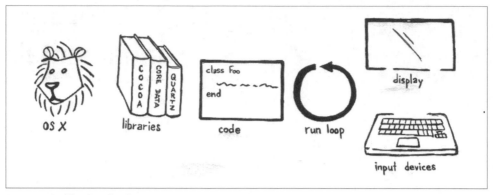

Figure 2-2. The details of a GUI app

Run Loops

The first challenge is that we don't want our code to execute and exit. We need our code to keep running to intercept my mom's actions and react to them. We can't pause or ask our code to sleep, because doing so might make us miss some events. Instead, we use what is called a *run loop*. Run loops are like threads that schedule work and coordinate the receipt of incoming events. By default, Cocoa applications have a main run loop that handles the events and keeps the application running. However, developers must be careful not to block this main loop, because that would prevent the user from interacting with the application and will cause the infamous spinning "pizza of death," aka "beach ball of death," to be displayed. To avoid that, you can use multiple run loops or, more simply, use asynchronous APIs.

Callbacks/Delegation

A *callback* is a function that you define but that is called by some other part of the system. Callbacks are the center of event-driven applications, which certainly include the ones you'll write for the Mac (and which also includes Ruby on Rails applications, with which you may be familiar). The runtime loop calls one of your functions when an event takes place you need to handle (Figure 2-3).

Asynchronous APIs also use callbacks. After you launch an asynchronous operation, your application continues while the operation takes place in the background. For instance, you may launch an operation that downloads a large file over the network while you allow the program to continue and handle other requests. This means that whatever code you want to execute at the successful completion of the operation—for instance, storing the file on the disk after it has been downloaded—has to be encapsulated in a callback, which the runtime invokes. Asynchronous operations also let you specify functions to be called in case of error and for other reasons. All these functions are called *delegate* callbacks.

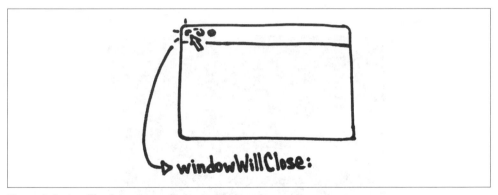

Figure 2-3. A callback is triggered when a window closes

Figure 2-3 shows a callback triggered when the user clicks on the Close button of a window. The callback is called only if you previously attached it to this instance of the window. You might have noticed that the callback selector ends with a colon, which means that it takes an argument (in this case a notification). We will discuss the call-back/notification concepts a bit further in Chapter 5.

User Inputs

User inputs, such as keyboard or mouse events, need to be wired to actions so that you, the developer, can decide what happens when an event is triggered. When developing Cocoa applications, this is usually done in Xcode's Interface Builder. The developer links an action received on a UI item to a controller's action.

Figure 2-4 shows the connections between a button and a controller. As you can see, the button's sent action (the action triggered when the button is clicked) is associated with the controller object. What that means is that when the button is pressed, the method calls `button_pressed` on the `Controller` class.

Figure 2-5 shows how the controller handles the connection from a button to an action. In the Received Actions list, notice that the button object's push button action is wired to the `button_pressed` action on the controller.

As a quick preview of what we will discuss later on, here is the only code required to implement a button action:

```
class Controller
  def button_pressed(sender)
    puts "The button was pressed"
  end
end
```

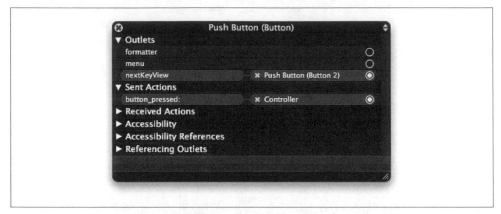

Figure 2-4. Button connections in Xcode

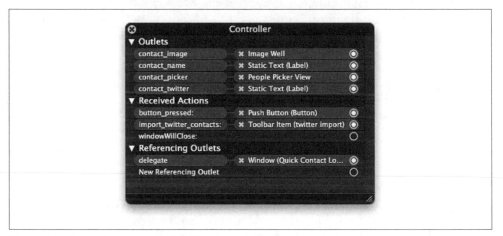

Figure 2-5. Controller connections in Xcode

The wiring itself is done graphically in Interface Builder: you create a controller object that you connect to the **Controller** class, drag a button from the library, visually link its action to your controller object, and choose the action to trigger. But I am getting ahead of myself—you will see that in a later chapter.

The point is that connecting user inputs to code is trivial with MacRuby.

Outlets

You might have noticed in the previous connection screenshots that some *outlets* were mentioned. Outlets keep track of UI elements such as windows and widgets in your code. In Figure 2-5, for instance, the controller defines four outlets to keep track of four UI elements used to display contact information.

Most of the time, you want to keep track of the application's state programmatically and make some modifications to UI objects. To do that you need a way to reference events, and that's what outlets are for. Creating an outlet in a class is very simple—just create an attribute accessor (technically a getter/setter to an instance variable):

```
class Controller
  attr_accessor :main_button
end
```

Once you have defined the outlet, Interface Builder automatically adds it to the list of available outlets, and you can connect a UI element to an outlet via Xcode's Interface Builder.

Again, you will see much more about the use of outlets later on. What is important to remember is that keeping track of UI elements from controllers is straightforward. When an event is triggered, your callback receives the notification and can modify the state of any UI element.

Display

So far, you have seen that the code runs continuously in a run loop, and waits for events. You saw that events can trigger actions and that action code has access to UI elements. The last missing piece is the rendering or display of data on the screen. Cocoa UIs are usually designed using Xcode, which comes with a library of UI elements ready to be used.

Figure 2-6 shows a sample of the various UI objects available to OS X developers.

To build your application UI, you can drag and drop the elements and connect them visually to the icons representing your code. Most elements know how to redraw themselves, so you don't need to do anything more. However, if you start doing anything advanced, such as developing video games or drawing on the screen, you might need to mark your elements as needing to be redrawn, or actually define how to redraw the elements. But we will keep that for later.

Example

If you have not used Cocoa previously, some of the concepts we've discussed might be a bit hard to grasp. Maybe the best way to bridge the gap is to jump ahead and take some time to just play with an application and look at how it works. We are going to write some example apps later on, but to get a feel for the meaning of everything we just discussed, download the demo application for this chapter (*https://github.com/ mattetti/MacRuby—The-Definitive-Guide*). Open it with Xcode (double-click *demo.xcodeproj*) and press Command-R (or click the Run button). Figure 2-7 shows how the running demo app should look.

Example | 25

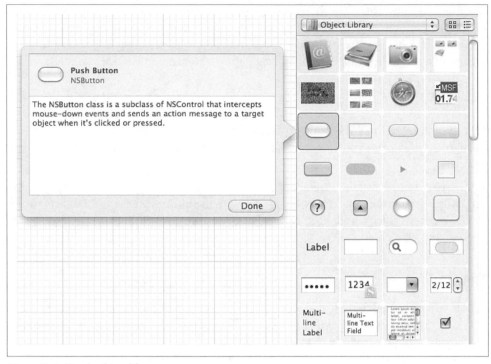

Figure 2-6. Xcode object library

 Make sure the "Demo" scheme is selected.

Take some time to play with the app: change the label text, turn on the mouse coordinate logger, apply some image filters, drag and drop another image, resize the window, and close the window or click the quit button. You might also want to look up the documentation for some of the APIs we are using, such as `NSWindow`.

Not all the concepts discussed here are shown in the demo app. My goal is to give you a quick idea of what you can do, how much code is needed, and how things connect to each other.

For a better understanding of how things work, focus on these two files:

* *controller.rb*
* *MainMenu.xib*

MainMenu.xib is the "view" file that defines all the UI elements and wires them to our code, which lives in the *controller.rb* file. At this point, I am not going to explain the code in detail, but the code can give you a feel for how things fit together.

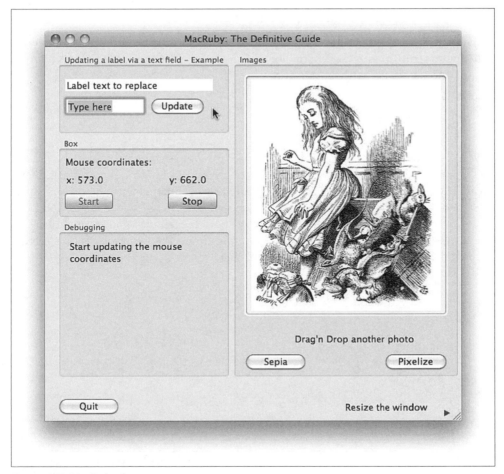

Figure 2-7. MacRuby demo app

This is just an example app, and it does not necessarily enforce best practices.

Start by opening the *MainMenu.xib* file. Now right-click the Window icon. You should see the window's delegate pointing to the controller object. Right-click the controller object and you will see all the outlets and actions.

Next, start inspecting some of these objects by opening the Utilities bar (View → Utilities → Attributes Inspector) and selecting some items. In parallel, open *controller.rb*. Look at how the outlets map to the attribute accessors (lines starting by `attr_accessor`) and at how the actions map to the methods taking an argument, such as

Example | 27

update_text_field. Delegate methods include windowShouldClose and windowDidResize. A timer runs without blocking the main loop.

Take some time to get familiar with the code. Try adding a new button and connecting it to a new action. Test the effect of blocking the main loop by adding a sleep call to an action, for instance, to the sepia action:

```
def sepia(sender)
  sleep(15) # block the main loop for 15 seconds
  # rest of the code
end
```

If you feel like playing and have some experience with Xcode, add more UI elements and figure out how to make them behave properly when the window is resized. Don't worry if you are not fully getting it yet. The next few chapters focus on how things are designed, which tools to use, and how to map your existing knowledge to MacRuby and Cocoa. After that, we will go back to concrete examples and examine how to accomplish specific tasks. Feel free to jump ahead and then come back to the more technical explanations if that works best for you.

## CHAPTER 3

The Cocoa Environment

Programmers who have written Mac OS X or iOS applications using Objective-C are already familiar with Cocoa and should recognize its APIs in the examples in Chapter 1, albeit with some odd syntax changes noted in that chapter. Ruby programmers who want an introduction to Cocoa can find it in this chapter. MacRuby lets you mix Ruby and Cocoa APIs seamlessly. But as you start developing Cocoa applications, you will start having to use Cocoa-specific APIs to solve Cocoa-specific challenges.

History

In the early 1980s, two engineers from the company StepStone, named Brad J. Cox and Tom Love, designed a C-based language inspired by SmallTalk-80. Their goal was to implement an object-oriented extension to the C language. The result was called Objective-C.

In 1985, Steve Jobs founded NeXT, a computer platform development company specializing in the higher education and business markets.

In 1988, NeXT licensed Objective-C from StepStone and wrote libraries and a compiler to build NeXTSTEP's user interface and interface builder. NeXTSTEP, NeXT's Unix-based operating system was particularly notable because of its focus on object-oriented programming and its many powerful toolkits.

Writing applications for NeXTSTEP was known to be far easier than on many competing systems. The UI was consistent and refined. Tim Berners-Lee, credited as the inventor of the World Wide Web, wrote the very first web browser, called WorldWideWeb (*http://www.w3.org/People/Berners-Lee/WorldWideWeb*), in 1990 on NeXT (Figure 3-1), and even claimed that he could not have done what he did as easily if he had to use other technologies.

> "I could do in a couple of months what would take more like a year on other platforms, because on the NeXT, a lot of it was done for me already."
>
> —Tim Berners-Lee, World Wide Web inventor

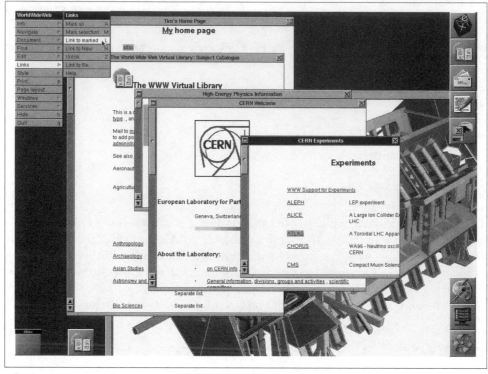

Figure 3-1. Screenshot of WorldWideWeb, the very first web browser

WorldWideWeb was not the only ground-breaking application developed on NeXT-STEP. Apple's Interface Builder, the initial implementations of Doom, Macromedia FreeHand, and Lotus Improv were also built on that platform.

In 1996, NeXT was acquired by Apple, which used parts from NeXTSTEP and from the open source Berkeley Software Distribution systems to build its new operating system: Mac OS X. The new OS included Objective-C as well as NeXT's developer and interface tools/frameworks, which became the base of the Cocoa API.

Main Frameworks in the Cocoa API

What's known as the Cocoa API is really a collection of several frameworks. More precisely, it is what is known as an "umbrella framework," a framework built up from other frameworks.

In this context, when we talk about frameworks, we are referring to application frameworks, which are usually a collection of advanced object-oriented APIs allowing software developers to work in a specific development environment.

Developers writing applications usually spend a lot of time coding the same features over and over: creating and managing a window, creating a menu and menu items, handling undos and redos, and so on.

Apple, and NeXTSTEP before them, saw the need to streamline the application development process. To do that, the two companies decided to provide developers with all the common features required to build Mac OS X applications. OS X developers can rely on these building blocks to focus on the unique values of their applications instead of constantly reinventing the wheel.

Cocoa takes advantage of common object-oriented design patterns and best practices identified and implemented by NeXTSTEP, resulting in a dynamic, mature, consistent, and extensive set of libraries.

The Cocoa API minimum set is an umbrella framework called `Cocoa.framework`. When loading this framework, you really load three Objective-C frameworks: `Foundation`, `AppKit,` and `CoreData`.

But more than a collection of APIs, the Cocoa framework enforces conventions when it comes to the UI. By using the APIs, you buy into Apple's view of how the user should see and interact with the device. These conventions also allow for tools such as Xcode to exist and to leverage APIs, while enforcing a consistent user experience.

 To use a class from one of these frameworks, you need to make sure to load the framework first. This is also true when using `macirb`. Each framework can be loaded individually without having to load the entire Cocoa framework. This can be interesting if you are developing an application that doesn't have a UI, such as a shared library or a script.

Foundation Framework

This is also known as the Foundation Kit. `Foundation` defines primitive object classes and data types such as strings, arrays, collection classes, dates, XML parser, notifications, IOs, iterators, and run loops. It is the base layer of the Objective-C classes (*http: //developer.apple.com/mac/library/documentation/cocoa/Reference/Foundation/ObjC _classic/Intro/IntroFoundation.html*).

The `Foundation` framework defines `NSObject` (the base Object class), as well as subclasses and constants prefixed by "NS" (standing variously for NextStep or NeXT/Sun). Later in this chapter, you will read about the essential classes defined by this framework.

AppKit Framework

This is also known as Application Kit (*http://developer.apple.com/mac/library/documen tation/cocoa/Reference/ApplicationKit/ObjC_classic/Intro/IntroAppKit.html*). `AppKit` is a direct descendant of the original NeXTSTEP Application Kit. It contains all the objects needed to implement graphical, event-driven UI objects, such as windows, panels, buttons, menus, scrollers, and text fields. The framework also handles screen drawing and refresh.

Basically, every time you write a GUI, you will use `AppKit`.

> If you are writing an OS X application that doesn't require a GUI or a data model based on CoreData, you don't have to load these Cocoa frameworks.

CoreData Framework

`CoreData` contains interfaces to manage your application's data model (*http://developer .apple.com/mac/library/referencelibrary/GettingStarted/GettingStartedWithCoreData*). Basically, it allows developers to deal easily with objects' life cycles and graph management. That includes validation, database object change tracking (undo, redo) and propagation, persistence, filtering, fetching, and Cocoa bindings.

In a nutshell, `CoreData` encapsulates the model in the MVC (model-view-controller) design pattern.

`CoreData` can be seen as an object-relational mapper (ORM) on steroids. Developers can choose one of the multiple data stores supported: XML, atomic (binary or custom), SQLite, and in-memory.

However, don't think that `CoreData` is restricted to database-oriented applications.

Reference Library

Apple's Reference Library will soon become your best friend. It describes all the Objective-C methods, C functions, and constants made available by the Cocoa API and other various related frameworks. Thanks to MacRuby, they are all accessible to you.

You can access this reference API offline by using Xcode, or online at *http://developer .apple.com*.

> The offline documentation is stored in the */Developer/Documentation/ DocSets* folder. Using the */Developer/usr/bin/docsetutil* utility command line, you can query the documentation. Writing a small application around the docsets can be a great way to get familiar with MacRuby and Cocoa.

After you connect to the Apple Developer Connection website, choose the Mac Dev Center. At this point, if you haven't created an account, you might want to sign up.

Signing up is free and will give you access to the latest version of the Xcode package, as well as some development videos.

In the Development Resources section of the page, you will find some sample code and training videos, but more important, the Mac Reference Library.

The library is maintained and kept up to date by Apple. You will notice that the documents are organized by types, topics, and frameworks. If you find a document that you are interested in, you can download it as a PDF to consult it later offline.

Let's do a search on NSDate and open the NSDate Class Reference page (Figure 3-2). API reference documents appear basically the same whether you view them online or via Xcode.

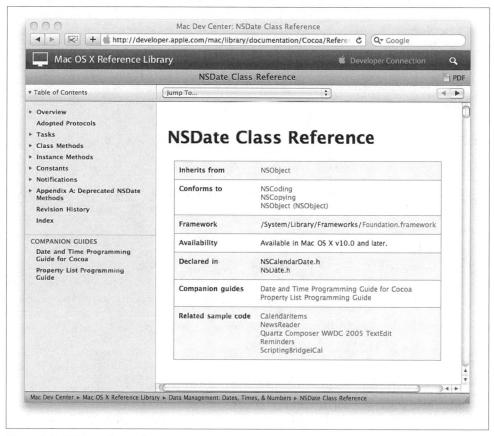

Figure 3-2. NSDate class reference

It's important to understand how the documentation is structured, so you can efficiently find the information you need when you need it.

Central Panel

Inherits from
> The inheritance tree of the class we are looking at. In this case, `NSDate` is a direct subclass of `NSObject`. Each class can inherit from only one parent, but the inheritance tree can go far back. If you look at `NSView`, for instance, you will notice that the inheritance tree is a bit longer: *NSResponder : NSObject*. This means that `NSView` is a subclass of `NSResponder`, which in turn is a subclass of `NSObject`. That means all methods, delegates, notifications, and constants of `NSResponder` and `NSObject` are available in `NSView`. Don't forget to browse superclasses when learning new classes.

Conforms to
> A list of protocols our class conforms to. It's basically a list of conventions and methods implemented by various other classes.

Framework
> The name of the framework defining the class.

Availability
> The OS versions supporting the class.

Declared in
> The header files defining the class. Not really useful for MacRuby developers, since we don't need to include any header files.

Companion guides
> A list of guides related to the class.

Related sample code
> A list of examples using the class in question. Most of these examples are in Objective-C, but since the API usage is the same, you should not have a problem reading them.

Sidebar

The sidebar lists links that cover all the aspects of the class.

In addition to the topics mentioned in the previous section, you will find a new listing. While some sections might be really obvious, some might be a bit more cryptic.

Tasks
> Lists class and instance methods by topic. This is particularly useful when you are reading the documentation of a class you don't know yet. Instead of trying to guess the name of the method, start with this section.

Notifications
The delegate methods triggered on class instances that implement these notification methods.

Mutability

Before looking a bit at some key Cocoa classes, we need to talk about *mutability*. By definition, an *immutable* object is an object whose state cannot be modified after being created. In contrast, a *mutable* object can be modified after creation.

Some Cocoa classes even come in two separate versions, mutable and immutable. Mutable classes descend from their nonmutable counterparts and therefore share the same methods. The main reason for having both classes is that immutable classes are optimized to be more efficient, based on the expectation that their contents are fixed:

```
framework 'foundation'
mutable_array = []          # => []
mutable_array << 'foo'      # => ["foo"]


immutable_array = NSArray.alloc.initWithArray(['foo', 'bar'])  # => ["foo", "bar"]
immutable_array << 'foo'  # RuntimeError: can't modify frozen/immutable array
```

 Something else to keep in mind when choosing a Cocoa class: Cocoa doesn't let you query whether you are dealing with a mutable or an immutable object. That may come as a surprise, but it's intended. Make sure to always pay attention to documentation for the APIs returning strings, arrays, hashes/dictionaries, and sets (NSArray, NSString, NSDictionary, and NSSet).

Ruby classes are usually mutable, but the state of a Ruby object can be *frozen*. In other words, in Ruby, you can make a mutable object immutable by freezing it. Cocoa accomplishes this by having two versions of a class, a mutable version and an immutable version:

```
my_string = "Understanding Ruby"
my_string.freeze
my_string.upcase! # => RuntimeError: can't modify frozen string

array = Array.new   # => []
array << 'foo'      # => ["foo"]

array.freeze
array << 'bar'      # RuntimeError: can't modify frozen/immutable array
```

Now it's time to get a quick tour of some of the classes you are going to encounter frequently.

## CHAPTER 4

Foundation

As stated in Chapter 3, Foundation defines the primitive object classes and data types used by all the other classes in Cocoa. It's therefore the first stop in our examination of frameworks for Cocoa and MacRuby.

Compatibility Table

When it comes to primitive types, MacRuby developers often have a choice between Cocoa Foundation classes and native Ruby classes. Before going through the list of key classes, their purposes, and how to use them, it is important understand the differences and relationships between Ruby primitives and Foundation primitives.

Table 4-1 shows classes that are implemented in such a way that the Ruby classes are compatible with their Foundation and Core Foundation counterparts.

Table 4-1. Ruby/Foundation/Core Foundation compatibility table

Ruby class	Compatible Foundation class	Compatible Core Foundation type
String	NSString/NSMutableString	CFString/CFMutableString
Array	NSArray/NSMutableArray	CFArray/CFMutableArray
Hash	NSDictionary/ NSMutableDictionary	CFDictionary/ CFMutableDictionary
Integer (Fixnum, Bignum)	NSNumber	CFNumber
Float	NSNumber	CFNumber
Time	NSDate	CFDate

Even though the Exception and NSException classes are not compatible per se, Ruby's syntax can rescue NSException instances, meaning that the developer can define a behavior in case a defined exception is caught.

This compatibility map is important because it means that even though a certain API might expect to receive an instance of NSArray, if you send it an instance of Array, everything will work as expected. Also, if an API returns an NSMutableDictionary instance, for example, the Hash instance methods can be used on the returned object. You can use any of the Hash or NSDictionary/NSMutableDictionary instance methods on the returned object.

However, some Ruby classes are not compatible with their Foundation equivalents and when using them in conjunction with other Cocoa libraries, one needs to be careful to use the appropriate class. Table 4-2 shows Ruby and Foundation classes that play similar roles but are *not* compatible.

Table 4-2. Incompatible types in Ruby and Cocoa frameworks

MacRuby class	Foundation counterparts
Set	NSSet, NSMutableSet, NSCountedSet, NSHashTable
Enumerator	NSEnumerator, NSFastEnumerationEnumerator
Date	NSDate, NSCalendar

This means if an API expects an object of a certain type, you can't provide it with a counterpart from the other column. For instance, if a Cocoa API expects an instance of NSDate, you can't pass it a Ruby date object. What you might want to do in such a case is convert an object as shown in "Date, Time, and Calendars" on page 43.

Now that we have this reference frame, let's look at the key classes defined by Foundation.

Strings and Attributed Strings

Cocoa's Foundation string class is NSString. MacRuby's String class is fully compatible with NSString/NSMutableString because NSString is "toll-free bridged" with its Core Foundation counterpart: CFString. In other words, whenever a method is expecting a String, NSString, or CFStringRef, you are free to use whichever class instance you want.

NSString and String have different APIs, but offer more or less the same features. Here are a few NSString methods that are not available in the traditional Ruby API but are quite useful nonetheless:

pathComponents
> Returns each path component of a path represented as a string:

```
>> framework 'Foundation'
=> true
>> "/Developer/Examples/Ruby/MacRuby".pathComponents
=> ["/", "Developer", "Examples", "Ruby", "MacRuby"]
```

pathExtension

Returns the extension of a path represented as a string:

```
>> framework 'Foundation'
=> true
file_path = "~/Music/born_to_be_alive.m4a"
file_path.pathExtension
# => "m4a"
# similar to Ruby's
File.extname(path)
# => ".m4a"
```

Attributed string objects, represented in Cocoa by `NSAttributedString`, manage sets of text attributes, such as font and kerning, that are associated with strings. `NSAttributedString` is not a subclass of `NSString`, but it does contain an `NSString` object to which it applies attributes. `NSAttributedString` supports HTML, Rich Text Format (including file attachments and graphics), drawing in `NSView` objects, and word and line calculation.

The `NSAttributedString` instance attributes are set/retrieved via a `Hash`:

```
>> framework 'Foundation'
=> true
font = NSFont.fontWithName("Helvetica", size:14.0)
content = "So Long, and Thanks for All the Fish"
attributes = {NSFontAttributeName => font}
attr_string = NSAttributedString.alloc.initWithString(content, attributes: attributes)
attr_string.string
# => "So Long, and Thanks for All the Fish"

total_range = NSMakeRange(0,attr_string.string.size)
attr_string.attributesAtIndex(0, effectiveRange: total_range)
=> {"NSFont"=>#<NSFont:0x20027d7c0>}
```

The AppKit framework also uses `NSParagraphStyle`/`NSMutableParagraphStyle` to encapsulate the paragraph or ruler attributes used by the `NSAttributedString` classes.

String instances are usually mutable (see "Mutability" on page 35 for details about mutability), but might be modified to become immutable.

Arrays

MacRuby's `Array` implementation is fully compatible with the mutable version of `NSArray`. That means that anywhere you need to use or pass a `NSMutableArray`, you can use an instance of `Array`, and vice versa.

Array instances are usually mutable (see "Mutability" on page 35 for details about mutability), but some APIs might modify a passed array to become immutable. Make sure you know which type you have.

Ruby's API is often easier to use and less verbose. For instance, here is how you create a new array instance using Cocoa's `NSMutableArray`:

```
>> framework 'Foundation'
# don't forget nil as the last element
>> NSArray.arrayWithObjects('so', 'say', 'we', 'all', nil)
=> ["so", "say", "we", "all"]
```

Here's the same thing using Ruby's syntax:

```
>> ["so", "say", "we", "all"]
=> ["so", "say", "we", "all"]
```

You can read more about Ruby's `Array` on Ruby's document website (*http://www .ruby -doc.org/core/classes/Array.html*).

The Ruby syntax creates mutable array versions by default, so if you receive an immutable version of an array and want a mutable version, you can use the `mutableCopy` method:

```
>> framework 'Foundation'
=> true
# create an immutable array
>> a = NSArray.arrayWithObjects('terrans', 'zerg', 'protoss', nil)
=> ["terrans", "zerg", "protoss"]
>> b = a.mutableCopy
=> ["terrans", "zerg", "protoss"]
>> b << "Xel'Naga"
=> ["terrans", "zerg", "protoss", "Xel'Naga"]
```

Conversely, if you want a copy of an mutable array to be immutable, use the `#copy` method available from `NSObject`:

```
>> array = ['M', 'V', 'C']
=> ["M", "V", "C"]
>> copy = array.copy
=> ["M", "V", "C"]
>> copy.class
=> Array
```

Another way to achieve the same result is to use Ruby's `dup` instance method.

Read the `NSCopying` and `NSMutableCopying` Protocol References for more information. These protocols are implemented by a majority of the Cocoa classes.

A few Foundation methods that have no counterparts in the traditional Ruby API can be very useful, including the following:

`firstObjectCommonWithArray`
> Returns the first object contained in the receiver that's equal to an object in another given array. For instance:
>
> ```
> >> [1,2,3].firstObjectCommonWithArray([3,4,5])
> => 3
> ```
>
> is the same as:

```
>> ([1,2,3] & [3,4,5]).first
=> 3
```

writeToFile:atomically

Writes the contents of the receiver to a file at a given path:

```
>> order = ['double double', ['pickles', 'onions'], {:animal_style => true}]
=> ["double double", ["pickles", "onions"], {:animal_style=>true}]
>> order.writeToFile("/tmp/in-n-out", atomically: true)
=> true
```

The array is serialized to disk using a property list, producing the following file:

```
<?xml version="1.0" encoding="UTF-8"?>
<!DOCTYPE plist PUBLIC "-//Apple//DTD PLIST 1.0//EN"
"http://www.apple.com/DTDs/PropertyList-1.0.dtd">
<plist version="1.0">
<array>
  <string>double double</string>
  <array>
    <string>pickles</string>
    <string>onions</string>
  </array>
  <dict>
    <key>animal_style</key>
    <true/>
  </dict>
</array>
</plist>
```

It can then be deserialized using the arrayWithContentsOfFile class method:

```
>> NSMutableArray.arrayWithContentsOfFile("/tmp/in-n-out")
=> ["double double", ["pickles", "onions"], {"animal_style"=>true}]
```

 This serialization process is fast and easy, but works with only a few basic types. For more general use, try other built-in serialization solutions such as YAML, JSON, marshaling, and a lower-level serialization provided by NSData.

Hashes/Dictionaries

MacRuby's Hash implementation is fully compatible with NSMutableDictionary, allowing you to use Ruby and Objective-C's methods on the same objects. Also, because NSDictionary is "toll-free bridged" with its Core Foundation counterpart, CFDictionary, the Core Foundation type is interchangeable in function or method calls with the bridged Foundation object. In other words, you can use MacRuby, Foundation, or Core Foundation hash/dictionaries interchangeably. If you are calling a C function that requires an instance of one of these dictionary classes, you can pass it a Hash instance, and it will work just fine.

Since `NSDictionary` object creation is different from its Ruby counterpart, let's compare both approaches:

Cocoa:

```
keys    = ['Matt', 'Laurent', 'Vincent']
objects = ['double-double', '3x3', 'cheeseburger']
NSMutableDictionary.dictionaryWithObjects(objects, forKeys:keys)
# => {"Matt"=>"double-double", "Laurent"=>"3x3", "Vincent"=>"cheeseburger"}
```

or:

```
NSMutableDictionary.dictionaryWithObjectsAndKeys(
        'double-double', 'Matt',
        '3x3', 'Laurent',
        'cheeseburger', 'Vincent', nil)
# => {"Matt"=>"double-double", "Laurent"=>"3x3", "Vincent"=>"cheeseburger"}
```

Ruby:

```
{"Matt"=>"double-double", "Laurent"=>"3x3", "Vincent"=>"cheeseburger"}
# => {"Matt"=>"double-double", "Laurent"=>"3x3", "Vincent"=>"cheeseburger"}
```

You can read more about Ruby's `Hash` on Ruby's document website (*http://www.ruby -doc.org/core/classes/hash.html*).

Just as with `NSArray`, Ruby's API is often easier to use. `NSDictionary` also implements serialization via `writeToURL:atomically:` and `NSDictionary.dictionaryWithContentsOf File`.

Sets

Ruby's `Set`, like Cocoa's `NSSet`, `NSMutableSet`, `NSCountedSet`, and `NSHashTable` classes, implements unordered collections of distinct elements. It might seem convenient to build MacRuby's `Set` on top of one of the Cocoa set classes, but it is actually implemented entirely from scratch. The main reason is that `NSSet` and its variants behave significantly differently from Ruby's `Set`. So look at the Cocoa and Ruby implementations and choose whichever one makes more sense for your case.

The name `NSHashTable` might lead you to believe the class is somehow related to Ruby's `Hash` class, but they are quite different, `NSHashTable` is a variant of `NSSet`. The big difference between `NSHashTable` and the other `Set` implementations is that `NSHashTable` supports weak references in a garbage-collected environment. Unless you have a very specific need for weak references, stick to Ruby or Cocoa's Set implementations.

Enumerators

`NSEnumerator` and `NSFastEnumerationEnumerator` are conceptually the same as Ruby `Enumerator`, except that the Ruby version is much more powerful.

The aim of these classes is to allow collections of objects, such as arrays, sets, and dictionaries/hashes, to be processed one at a time.

When using the Ruby API, just pass a block (an anonymous method) to one of the many collection methods that return an enumerator:

```
["Eloy", "Matthias", "Joshua", "Thibault"].each do |name|
  puts "#{name} is a great developer!"
end
# => Eloy is a great developer!
# => Matthias is a great developer!
# => Joshua is a great developer!
# => Thibault is a great developer!
["Eloy", "Matthias", "Joshua", "Thibault"]
```

The array is being enumerated and each item is sent to the block.

You can also get an `Enumerator` instance and store it in a variable to call methods on it later on:

```
object_enumerator = {'nl' => "Eloy",
                     'ch' => "Matthias",
                     'us' => "Joshua",
                     'fr' => "Thibault"}.each_value
object_enumerator.each_slice(2) do |name_1, name_2|
  puts "#{name_1} and #{name_2}"
end

# outputs
Thibault and Matthias
Eloy and Joshua
```

Date, Time, and Calendars

Cocoa and MacRuby provide much more sophisticated time options than simple time-stamps or even date/time formatting routines.

NSDate

`NSDate` is the class that implements dates and times in Cocoa. It is used to create date objects and perform date-based calculations. `NSDate` objects are invariant points in time and therefore immutable:

```
now = NSDate.date
now.description
# => "2009-12-30 23:09:16 -0500"

seconds_per_day = 24 * 60 * 60
tomorrow = NSDate.alloc.initWithTimeIntervalSinceNow(seconds_per_day)
tomorrow.description
# => "2009-12-31 23:09:27 -0500"

NSDate.date
```

```
# => 2009-12-30 23:10:02 -0500
NSDate.dateWithTimeIntervalSinceNow(10.0)
# => 2009-12-30 23:10:12 -0500
```

NSDate also has more flexible ways to create dates, for instance:

```
framework 'Foundation'
NSDate.dateWithNaturalLanguageString('next Tuesday dinner').description
# =>"2010-01-12 19:00:00 -0800"

NSDate.dateWithString("2010-01-10 23:51:05 -0800").description
=> "2010-01-10 23:51:05 -0800"

date_string = "3pm June 30, 2010"
NSDate.dateWithNaturalLanguageString(date_string).description
# => "2010-06-30 15:00:00 -0700"
NSDate.dateWithNaturalLanguageString("06/30/2010").description
# => "2010-06-30 12:00:00 -0700"
```

Here is the Ruby API to create Time instances:

```
>> Time.now
# => 2009-12-30 23:19:00 -0500
>> Time.now + (24 * 60 * 60)
# => 2009-12-31 23:19:00 -0500
```

Ruby's date and time APIs are usually more flexible than their Cocoa counterparts. However, some Cocoa APIs expect NSDate instances and, in some cases, Ruby's API lacks some features. Being familiar with Cocoa's date and time management is therefore important.

If you want to convert an instance of Time and to an NSDate instance, use NSDate.date WithString and pass it the string representation of your time object. For example:

```
NSDate.dateWithString(Time.now.to_s)
```

NSCalendar

The NSCalendar class represents calendar objects and covers the most used calendars—Buddhist, Gregorian, Hebrew, Islamic, and Japanese:

```
current_calendar = NSCalendar.currentCalendar
```

Calendars are used in conjunction with NSDateComponents and NSDate:

```
today      = NSDate.date
calendar   = NSCalendar.currentCalendar
units      = (NSDayCalendarUnit | NSWeekdayCalendarUnit)
components = calendar.components(units, fromDate: today)
components.day     # => 30
components.weekday # => 4
```

Consult the reference documentation about the available NSCalendarUnit constants to set the different units you might need. If you are using the Gregorian calendar, you can more easily access most of the date information using the strftime method of Ruby's

Time class. However, the Cocoa API is great for getting localized date management and access data unavailable in Ruby's API, such as era and quarter.

Data

The NSData and NSMutableData classes are typically used for data storage. NSData is "toll-free bridged" with its Core Foundation counterpart: CFData. This means the Core Foundation type is interchangeable with the bridged Foundation object in function or method calls. If a function expects a CFDataRef parameter, you can send it an NSData instance, and vice versa.

If you have a string and you want to access its data representation, use the dataUsingEncoding method:

```
string = "Some classes gets initiated using data, (i.e NSXMLDocument)"
data = string.dataUsingEncoding(NSUTF8StringEncoding)
# => #<NSConcreteMutableData:0x200295cc0>
```

Conversely, if you have some data and want to access a string representation, use the following:

```
NSString.alloc.initWithData(data, encoding:NSUTF8StringEncoding)
# => "Some classes gets initiated using data, (i.e NSXMLDocument)"
```

Quite often, when I have to deal with a lot of string/data conversions, I reopen the String and Data classes and add some conversion methods:

```
class String
  def to_utf8_data
    self.dataUsingEncoding(NSUTF8StringEncoding)
  end
end

class NSData
  def to_utf8_string
    NSString.alloc.initWithData(self, encoding:NSUTF8StringEncoding)
  end
end

"Can't wait until Taco Tuesday!".to_utf8_data
# => #<NSConcreteMutableData:0x2002ac400>
data.to_utf8_string
=> "Can't wait until Taco Tuesday!"
```

 In "Syntactic Sugar" on page 18 you saw that String instances respond to #to_data and NSData instances respond to #to_str. However, these methods encode the data using ASCII 8-bit instead of UTF-8, and sometimes you need the wider range of characters provided by UTF-8.

Locales

NSLocale, as its name implies, helps developers deal with different languages and linguistic, cultural, and technological conventions and standards. Using NSLocale, you can retrieve the system and/or user locale and load any of the available locales.

In addition to providing you with the user country and language codes, locales are very useful for displaying all sorts of localized data (time, date, monetary amounts, dimensions, etc.). Locales store information such as symbols used for the decimal separator in numbers, the way dates are formatted, and more:

```
framework 'Foundation'

locale = NSLocale.currentLocale
locale.objectForKey(NSLocaleLanguageCode)
# => "en"

# We could also use the MacRuby alias
locale[NSLocaleLanguageCode]
# => "en"

locale[NSLocaleCurrencyCode]
# => "USD"

locale[NSLocaleCurrencySymbol]
# => "$"

locale[NSLocaleUsesMetricSystem]
=> false

locale[NSLocaleCalendar].calendarIdentifier
=> "gregorian"

french_locale = NSLocale.alloc.initWithLocaleIdentifier("fr_FR")
french_locale.displayNameForKey(NSLocaleIdentifier, value: "en_US")
# => "anglais (États-Unis)"
```

 MacRuby adds some shortcuts/aliases to improve some of Cocoa's APIs. For instance, if an object responds to objectForKey: and setObject:forKey: you can use [] and []= instead. This is exactly what we did in the previous example. Writing locale[NSLocaleLanguage Code] has exactly the same effect as writing locale.objectForKey(NSLo caleLanguageCode).

Time Zones

NSTimeZone will provide you with all the information you need to handle timezones:

```
time_zone = NSTimeZone.localTimeZone
time_zone.name
# => "America/Los_Angeles"
```

```
time_zone.abbreviation
# => "PST"

time_zone.secondsFromGMT
=> -28800

time_zone.daylightSavingTime?
# same as calling time_zone.isDaylightSavingTime
=> false

french_locale = NSLocale.alloc.initWithLocaleIdentifier("fr_FR")
time_zone.localizedName(NSTimeZoneNameStyleStandard, locale: french_locale)
# => "heure normale du Pacifique"
```

Exceptions

Cocoa's NSException works the same as Ruby's Exception. As the following example shows, raised NSException instances can be caught by the standard Ruby syntax:

```
exception = NSException.exceptionWithName('MacRuby Book',
                                          reason: 'documentation purposes',
                                          userInfo: nil)
begin
  exception.raise
rescue Exception => e
  puts e.message
end
# => MacRuby Book: documentation purposes
```

I/O

As with most of the tasks discussed in this chapter, input and output (I/O) operations can be performed using either the Ruby or the Cocoa API. However, Cocoa will more than likely make your applications more robust and efficient, mainly because a lot of its APIs are asynchronous. Asynchronous APIs are important when writing desktop/mobile applications, because you don't want to block the main application process while waiting for your I/O operation to finish.

Let's imagine that you have a Twitter client and want to fetch the latest updates. If you don't use an asynchronous API, when the user clicks the refresh button, the application will freeze and the "beach volleyball/pizza of death" will spin until the API response is received from Twitter. To ensure a better user experience, it is recommended that you use an asynchronous API and provide some sort of indication of progress.

URLs/Requests/Connections

The NSURL, NSURLRequest, and NSURLConnection classes provide developers with ways to manipulate and load URLs and the resources they reference.

An NSURL object can refer to a local or remote resource. It's the recommended way to refer to files. Various protocols are supported:

- File Transfer Protocol (ftp://)
- Hypertext Transfer Protocol (http://)
- Secure 128-bit Hypertext Transfer Protocol (https://)
- Local file URLs (file://)

NSURL also transparently supports both proxy servers and SOCKS gateways using the user's system preferences.

Since NSURL is a class you will more than likely use often, let's start by covering some of the frequently used methods:

NSURL.fileURLWithPath
> Initializes and returns a newly created NSURL object as a file URL with a specified path:

```
framework 'Foundation'
url = NSURL.fileURLWithPath("/usr/local/bin/macruby")
url.description
# => "file://localhost/usr/local/bin/macruby"
```

isFileReferenceURL *or* fileReferenceURL?
> Returns True if the NSURL object refers to a file, false otherwise:

```
framework 'Foundation'
macruby = NSURL.fileURLWithPath("/usr/local/bin/macruby")
website = NSURL.URLWithString("http://macruby.org")

macruby.fileReferenceURL?
# => true
website.fileReferenceURL?
# => false
```

 MacRuby adds some syntactic sugar. Objective-C methods with an is prefix are aliased in MacRuby by adding a question mark at the end of the method name. For instance, an Objective-C method called isOpaque is also available in MacRuby using the opaque? method alias.

NSURL.URLWithString

Creates and returns an NSURL object initialized with the string provided. Here is an example with some of the available accessors. Refer to the API documentation for more details:

```
framework 'Foundation'
url = NSURL.URLWithString("http://macruby.org/downloads.html#beta")
# => #<NSURL:0x200262ba0>
url.absoluteString
# => "http://macruby.org/downloads.html#beta"
url.fragment
# => "beta"
url.host
# => "macruby.org"
url.path
# => "/downloads.html"
url = NSURL.URLWithString
("http://macruby.org/downloads.html?sorted=true&nightly=false")
url.query
# => "sorted=true&nightly=false"
url = NSURL.URLWithString("http://mattetti:apple@macruby.org:8888/admin")
url.port
# => 8888
url.user
# => "mattetti"
url.password
# => "apple"
```

The following list explains the methods used in the example. The different parts of a URL are defined by RFC 1808 (*http://www.ietf.org/rfc/rfc1808.txt*):

absoluteString

Returns a string representation of the URL.

fragment

Returns the fragment of the URL following a pound or hash sign.

host

Returns the URL's host.

path

Returns the URL's path.

query

Returns the query from the URL, the part following a question mark.

port

Returns the port from the URL.

user

Returns the user from the URL.

password

Returns the password from the URL.

`NSURLRequest` and `NSMutableURLRequest` objects represent URL load requests. These objects contain two different aspects of a load request: the URL to load and the cache policy to use. Once a URL request is defined, it can be loaded and processed using `NSURLConnection` or `NSURLDownload`.

The concepts in the following subsections apply to both `NSURLRequest` and `NSMutableURLRequest`, but for the sake of simplicity I'll refer just to `NSURLRequest`.

Cache Policy and Cache Access

Caching allows better performance and optimized resource usage. Of the standard protocols, `NSURLConnection` caches only HTTP and HTTPS requests, but custom protocols can also provide caching. `NSURLRequest` relies on a composite on-disk and in-memory cache, which is enabled by default.

Here is an example where we are sending a request to the MacRuby website ignoring any cached data:

```
framework 'Foundation'
url = NSURL.URLWithString('http://macruby.org')
request = NSMutableURLRequest.requestWithURL(url,
                  cachePolicy:NSURLRequestReloadIgnoringCacheData,
                  timeoutInterval:30.0)

NSURLConnection.connectionWithRequest(request, delegate:self)
puts "Connecting to http://macruby.org"

# response callback
def connection(connection, didReceiveResponse:response)
  puts "response received with status code: #{response.statusCode}"
  exit
end

# Keep the main loop running
NSRunLoop.currentRunLoop.runUntilDate(NSDate.distantFuture)
```

Unless specified otherwise, HTTP requests use the default HTTP cache protocol, which will cache them and use their ETag and Last-Modified headers to determine whether subsequent requests are stale. Using the headers, the cache is evaluated for each request. Read more about HTTP caching in RFC 2616 (*http://www.w3.org/Protocols/rfc2616/ rfc2616-sec13.html*) to see how to take advantage of this feature.

`NSURLConnection` allows you to alter default caching behavior. Four types of caching are available and can be passed as an argument:

Default cache policy (`NSURLRequestUseProtocolCachePolicy`*)*
    The default policy is specific to the protocol used and is the best conforming policy for the protocol.

Disabled cache policy (`NSURLRequestReloadIgnoringCacheData`*)*
    This ignores the cache, disabling it.

Use cached data, fallback on loading the resource (NSURLRequestReturnCacheDataElse
Load)

> Use of the cache can be forced, ignoring cache data age and expiration date. The request is loaded from its source only if no cache data is available. The data is also cached after it is loaded.

Offline mode (NSURLRequestReturnCacheDataDontLoad)

> This caching policy simulates an offline mode and loads data only from the cache.

NSURLDownload does not cache responses.

 Defining a request using NSURLRequest.requestWithURL uses the default cache policy and a default timeout of 30 seconds. But, of course, you can specify your own settings using NSRequest.requestWithURL:cachePo licy:timeoutInterval:.

Asynchronous Versus Synchronous

We have already touched briefly on the topic of asynchronous versus synchronous APIs. Ruby I/O APIs are synchronous, meaning that when an operation is performed, the process is blocked, waiting for the operation to be done. Blocking a process may not always be a problem. Separate threads can also be started to handle blocking I/Os.

When writing a web application, your application reacts to an action triggered by a user. If there is no traffic on your website, your code is idle. However, when writing a desktop or mobile application, your code is constantly running without requiring user interaction. To keep running, the application has a main run loop that keeps the code running. Within the run loops, you can use asynchronous APIs. Basically, you initiate an operation, return to other activities (or wait for further user input), and receive notification when the operation is done. To get the notification, you implement delegate methods and point to them when initiating the asynchronous operation.

If you are satisfied using synchronous APIs, stick to the Ruby standard libraries such as net/http or the methods available on NSString or NSData, as shown here:

```
framework 'Foundation'
url = NSURL.URLWithString 'http://macruby.org'
content = NSMutableString.alloc.initWithContentsOfURL(url,
                                         encoding:NSUTF8StringEncoding,
                                         error:nil)
```

or:

```
require 'net/http'
content = Net::HTTP.get('www.macruby.org', '/')
```

However, you will probably be more interested in using the asynchronous APIs provided by Cocoa. As an example, I'll discuss the NSURLDownload call mentioned in the previous section, which downloads remote content to file.

NSURLDownload downloads requests asynchronously. The request's body is saved into a file. When initiating the download, you specify the destination path and the delegator object containing the callbacks you want to use during the download. Within the delegator object, you can define a rich set of optional methods to check on redirection, download status, authentication challenges, and completion. These run automatically as the Cocoa runtime detects events. You can also cancel the load if needed.

Here is a sample download script. It starts by defining a class arbitrarily named DownloadDelegator. I've chosen to define four methods, including two variants of download. After defining the class, the script initiates a download by creating an object of type NSURLDownload. The runtime takes care of the rest, calling downloadDidBegin and downloadDidFinish at the appropriate moments.

The two download methods are defined on the DownloadDelegator class. They follow the delegate method signature defined by the NSURLDownload API. When we create our NSURLDownload instance, we also create an instance of DownloadDelegator, which we assign as a delegate object. This way the NSURLDownload instance will automatically try to dispatch the delegate methods if they are available on the delegate object. The download methods are then called automatically:

```
framework 'Cocoa'

class DownloadDelegator

  def downloadDidBegin(dl_process)
    puts "downloading..."
  end

  def download(dl_process, decideDestinationWithSuggestedFilename:filename)
    home = NSHomeDirectory()
    path = home.stringByAppendingPathComponent('Desktop')
    path = path.stringByAppendingPathComponent(filename)
    dl_process.setDestination(path, allowOverwrite:true)
  end

  def download(dl_process, didFailWithError:error)
    error_description = error.localizedDescription
    more_details      = error.userInfo[NSErrorFailingURLStringKey]
    puts "Download failed. #{error_description} - #{more_details}"
    exit
  end

  def downloadDidFinish(dl_process)
    puts "Download finished!"
    exit
  end

end

url_string = 'http://www.macruby.org/files/nightlies/macruby_nightly-latest.pkg'
url        = NSURL.URLWithString(url_string)
req        = NSURLRequest.requestWithURL(url)
```

```
file_download = NSURLDownload.alloc.initWithRequest(req,
                             delegate: DownloadDelegator.new)

# keep the run loop running
NSRunLoop.currentRunLoop.runUntilDate(NSDate.distantFuture)
```

Pipes

In Unix-like computer operating systems, pipes allow you to chain processes. The output of a process (`stdout`) feeds directly the input (`stdin`) of another one.

The `NSPipe` class provides an interface for accessing pipes. An `NSPipe` class instance represents both ends of a pipe and enables communication through the pipe.

File handles are used in the `NSTask` example a bit later in this chapter. Look at the example's code to learn how to create and monitor pipes.

File Handles

The `NSFileHandle` class provides a wrapper for accessing open files or communications channels. File handles can be retrieved for a URL, a path, standard input, standard output, standard error, or a null device. Some objects, such as pipes, also expose a file handle. Using a file handle, one can read or write the data source it references asynchronously.

File handles are used in the `NSTask` example a bit later in this chapter. Look at the example's code to learn how to use file handles.

Bundles

A *bundle* is a collection of code and resources used by an application, generally created outside the application. Bundles are usually built with Xcode using the Application or Framework project types, or using plug-ins. In most cases, your application bundle will contain *.nib*/*.xib* files, media assets (images/sounds), dynamic libraries, and frameworks. The `NSBundle` class creates objects that represent bundles.

Useful methods include:

`NSBundle.mainBundle`
> A class method returning the `NSBundle` object that usually corresponds to the application file package or application wrapper (the *.app* folder holding your code).

`localizations`
> Returns a list of all the localizations available in the bundle:
> ```
> framework 'Foundation'
> NSBundle.mainBundle.localizations
> # => ['English', 'French']
> ```

localizedStringForKey:value:table:
> Returns the localized version of a string from the *Localizable.strings* file.

pathForResource:ofType:
> Returns the full pathname for the resource identified by the specified name and file extension.

The following example registers a custom font (*akaDylan.ttf*) that was added to the resources folder. We can use it in our UI without having to install it on the user's machine:

```
framework 'Foundation'
font_location = NSBundle.mainBundle.pathForResource('akaDylan', ofType: 'ttf')
font_url = NSURL.fileURLWithPath(font_location)
# using this Core Text Font Manager function to register the embedded font.
CTFontManagerRegisterFontsForURL(font_url, KCTFontManagerScopeProcess, nil)
```

Scheduling

The OS X runtime offers both low-level threads and a collection of convenient ways to schedule activities such as timers and operation queues. We'll look at the various options in this section.

Run Loops

Run loops process input from the mouse, keyboard events from the window system, NSPort objects, NSConnection objects, NSTimer events, and other sources. Run loops are essential to keeping your application running and handling inputs. In Cocoa, the NSRunLoop class implements the run loop concept.

You don't need to create or manage NSRunLoop instances. Every NSThread object you create is already attached to its own NSRunLoop instance.

We've already used NSRunLoop in many of the examples in this chapter. What we did was retrieve the current thread's run loop and force it to run until a distant date:

```
framework 'Foundation'

future = NSDate.distantFuture
NSRunLoop.currentRunLoop.runUntilDate(future)
```

The most interesting methods provided by NSRunLoop are:

NSRunLoop.currentRunLoop
> As already shown, this returns the NSRunLoop object for the current thread. If a run loop does not yet exist, one is created and returned.

NSRunLoop.mainRunLoop
> Returns the run loop of the main thread.

currentMode

> Run loops can run in different modes, each of which defines its own set of objects to monitor. This method returns the run loop's input mode.

runUntilDate

> Runs the run loop for a delimited amount of time. More exactly, it sets the run loop to run until a specific date.

Timers

Sometimes you might want to trigger a method to run at a regular interval. For instance, you might want to redraw a video game screen 30 times a second or call an API every 2 minutes to check the status of a service. To do that, you can use a timer object defined by the NSTimer class.

Timers can be repeated or run once. If it's a repeating timer, it sends a specified method to a target object again and again based on the defined time interval.

Here is an example of a game loop implementation based on NSTimer:

```
framework 'Foundation'

class GameLoop

  def start
    @timer = NSTimer.scheduledTimerWithTimeInterval 0.06,
                                          target: self,
                                          selector: 'refresh_screen:',
                                          userInfo: nil,
                                          repeats: true
  end

  def refresh_screen(timer)
    puts "refresh"
  end

  def stop_refreshing
    @timer.invalidate && @timer = nil if @timer
  end

end

GameLoop.new.start
NSRunLoop.currentRunLoop.runUntilDate(NSDate.distantFuture)
```

NSTimer instances can fire only when the run loop they live in is running. Also, you need to keep in mind that the effective resolution of a timer is approximately 50 to 100 milliseconds. This should be fine for UI-driven interactive applications that don't depend on finer-grained execution times.

There are three ways to schedule a timer. The first is to use the following:

```
NSTimer.scheduledTimerWithTimeInterval:invocation:repeats:
```

or:

```
NSTimer.scheduledTimerWithTimeInterval:target:selector:userInfo:repeats:
```

This method creates the timer and schedules it on the current run loop in the default mode.

This method relies on the additional NSInvocation class, so to keep things simpler, let's look at an example using a second approach:

```
framework 'Foundation'

def do_something(timer)
  puts 'Do something'
end

NSTimer.scheduledTimerWithTimeInterval 0.06,
                        target: self,
                        selector: 'do_something:',
                        userInfo: nil,
                        repeats: true

NSRunLoop.currentRunLoop.runUntilDate(NSDate.distantFuture)
```

The first argument is the time interval, so in this case, the timer is going to fire 15 times a second (every 0.06 seconds). When the timer is triggered, it will send the do_something: selector to self (target:) and will pass a nil argument (specified by userInfo:). The timer will be repeated indefinitely.

 Selectors represent methods. A selector is just a string consisting of the method name followed by a colon.

You can pass any object to the method triggered by the timer. To do so, just pass your object via the userInfo argument. If you have multiple items of data to pass, combine them in an array or object. To retrieve the passed data, call #userInfo on the timer object passed to the callback.

The following is an example of a timer that fires just once:

```
framework 'Foundation'

def do_something(timer)
  puts "#{timer.userInfo} says: do something!"
  exit
end

NSTimer.scheduledTimerWithTimeInterval 0.5,
                        target: self,
                        selector: 'do_something:',
                        userInfo: 'Simon',
                        repeats: false
```

```
NSRunLoop.currentRunLoop.runUntilDate(NSDate.distantFuture)

# outputs:
# => 'Simon says: do something!'
```

Notice that the `userInfo` object is evaluated only the first time it's called. The following contrived example should make that clear. No matter when the timer runs, the `do_something` prints just the time that was stored in its argument the first time it ran:

```
framework 'Foundation'

def do_something(timer)
  puts timer.userInfo
end

NSTimer.scheduledTimerWithTimeInterval 0.5,
                        target: self,
                        selector: 'do_something:',
                        userInfo: Time.now,
                        repeats: true

NSRunLoop.currentRunLoop.runUntilDate(NSDate.distantFuture)

# outputs:
# => 2010-01-10 23:05:45 -0800
# => 2010-01-10 23:05:45 -0800
# => 2010-01-10 23:05:45 -0800
# => 2010-01-10 23:05:45 -0800
# => 2010-01-10 23:05:45 -0800
# [...]
```

Another option is to create a timer and not schedule it to a run loop right away. Do this using one of the following calls:

```
NSTimer.timerWithTimeInterval:invocation:repeats:a
NSTimer.timerWithTimeInterval:target:selector:userInfo:repeats:
```

After the timer is created, you must add it to a run loop using the `NSRunLoop`'s `add Timer:forMode:` method. For example:

```
framework 'Foundation'

def do_something(timer)
  puts 'do something'
end

timer = NSTimer.timerWithTimeInterval 0.5,
                        target: self,
                        selector: 'do_something:',
                        userInfo: nil,
                        repeats: true

# the timer isn't scheduled yet
# let's schedule it:
```

```
NSRunLoop.currentRunLoop.addTimer(timer, forMode: NSDefaultRunLoopMode)
NSRunLoop.currentRunLoop.runUntilDate(NSDate.distantFuture)
```

Finally, you can create a timer with a defined fire date and then attach it to a run loop:

```
framework 'Foundation'

def do_something(timer)
  puts 'do something'
  exit
end

in_2_seconds = Time.now + 2
timer = NSTimer.alloc.initWithFireDate NSDate.dateWithString(in_2_seconds.to_s),
                        interval: 0.5,
                        target: self,
                        selector: 'do_something:',
                        userInfo: nil,
                        repeats: false

NSRunLoop.currentRunLoop.addTimer(timer, forMode: NSDefaultRunLoopMode)
NSRunLoop.currentRunLoop.runUntilDate(NSDate.distantFuture)
```

Tasks/Subprocesses

You might want to run another program as a subprocess and monitor its execution. An easy way to do that is to use Ruby's API to shell out and call a program:

```
puts `/bin/ls -la /`
```

The back ticks execute the command, which is then printed. While this is very easy and nice, it blocks the main loop. So, if we were to start, for instance, an encoding process, we would have to wait for it to finish before we could continue the execution of our program. Not always ideal.

This is exactly when Cocoa's NSTask class shines. NSTask objects create separate executable entities. You can monitor the execution of your task using observers.

An NSTask needs to be passed a command to execute, the directory in which to run the task, and optional standard input/output/error values. An NSTask instance can be run only once. Subsequent attempts to run the task will raise an exception.

Here is an example showing how to asynchronously start a new process and monitor it:

```
framework 'Foundation'

class AsyncHandler
  def data_ready(notification)
    data = notification.userInfo[NSFileHandleNotificationDataItem]
    output = NSString.alloc.initWithData(data, encoding: NSUTF8StringEncoding)
    puts output
  end
  def task_terminated(notification)
    exit
  end
```

```
end

notification_handler = AsyncHandler.new
nc = NSNotificationCenter.defaultCenter

task = NSTask.alloc.init
pipe_out = NSPipe.alloc.init

task.arguments = ['-la']
task.currentDirectoryPath = "/"
task.launchPath       = "/bin/ls"
task.standardOutput = pipe_out
file_handle = pipe_out.fileHandleForReading

nc.addObserver(notification_handler,
              selector: "data_ready:",
              name: NSFileHandleReadCompletionNotification,
              object: file_handle)

nc.addObserver(notification_handler,
              selector: "task_terminated:",
              name: NSTaskDidTerminateNotification,
              object: task)

file_handle.readInBackgroundAndNotify
task.launch

# keep the run loop running
NSRunLoop.currentRunLoop.runUntilDate(NSDate.distantFuture)
```

We start by defining an `AsyncHandler` class that implements some callback methods (`data_ready` and `task_terminated`). We then create our task and a pipe to monitor the output of the task. Finally, we add an observer on the pipe's file handle (so we'll know when data is being written to it) and another notification (so we'll know when the task is done running). These observers invoke the callback methods we defined at the start.

The task is executed and the output is printed as it is pushed by the notification system. Once the task is done running, the program exits.

Threads

Threads are often used to run code that might take some time to execute, when the developer doesn't want to block the execution of the rest of the application.

In the case of a Cocoa application, the main thread handles the UI and the various inputs (user, network, devices, etc.). Using threads leaves the main thread to run smoothly while lengthy processing runs separately.

Using multiple threads can also distribute the load to multiple cores and therefore improve the performance of your code when run on multicore machines.

OS X uses POSIX threads, which are a standard seen on many Unix-type systems. But Cocoa has enhanced these threads to use a simple locking mechanism, NSLock. You can create threads using Cocoa's NSThread class or Ruby's Thread. Ruby's Thread class creates only POSIX threads, while NSThread creates Cocoa's enhanced threads by default, with the option of creating POSIX threads.

The only "inconvenience" with using POSIX threads is that unless you start an NSThread instance, Cocoa frameworks will think you are running in a single-threaded mode. This was historically important to optimize threaded versus nonthreaded code path, but nowadays the difference is not very important.

 It's fine to mix Cocoa threads and POSIX threads, but make sure to use their respective mutex classes to lock them.

An NSThread can be initiated with a target and method to call on it. Here is an example showing how to start an expensive process without blocking the main thread:

```
framework 'Foundation'

class ExpensiveCalculation
  def start(to_process)
    puts "processing on a separate thread"
    sleep(2)
    puts "processing is over"
  end
end

calculation = ExpensiveCalculation.new
thread = NSThread.alloc.initWithTarget( calculation,
                                        selector:'start:',
                                        object:'dummy_obj' )
thread.start
puts "the main thread is not blocked"

NSRunLoop.currentRunLoop.runUntilDate(NSDate.dateWithTimeIntervalSinceNow(3.0))
```

The output will be something like the following. The order of statements may be different, because the order in which the main thread and subordinate thread run is unpredictable:

```
processing on a separate thread
the main thread is not blocked
processing is over
```

Once you have an NSThread instance, you can also ask for its status:

```
framework 'Foundation'
thread = NSThread.alloc.init
thread.start

thread.cancelled?
```

```
# => false
thread.executing?
# => false
thread.finished?
# => true
```

MacRuby developers might, however, prefer to use Ruby's Thread API or Grand Central Dispatch (GCD).

As mentioned earlier, MacRuby's Thread class creates POSIX threads. The API is very simple:

```
def print_char(char)
  1.upto(5_000) do
    print char
  end
end

Thread.new{print_char('1')}
print_char('0')
```

The output will look more or less like the following:

```
# [..]
000000000000011111111111111111111111111111111111111111111111111111111111111
111111111101111111101111111111111100111111111111111001111111111111111001111111111111111
011111101111111111111100111111111111111100000000000000000000000000000000000000000000000
000000000000000000000000000000000000000000000000000000000000000000000000000011
111110111111111111111111001111111111111111001111110111111111011111111111111111000000000000
000000000000000000000000000000000000000000000000000000000001111111111111111
111111111111111111111111111111111111111111111111111111111111111111111111111111111111111111
# [..]
```

You can also pass a variable to a thread as follows:

```
['Joshua', 'Laurent', 'Matt'].each do |dev_name|
  Thread.new(dev_name){|name| puts "Hello, #{name}!\n"}
end
```

Each thread has access to its own local variable called name.

 MacRuby has been specifically designed with concurrency in mind. Unlike the main Ruby interpreter, threads are executed in parallel and multiple threads can concurrently call into MacRuby without blocking.

Operations/Operation Queues

Dealing with threads can be quite cumbersome and difficult. Thankfully, Cocoa encapsulates threads by grouping work that you want to perform asynchronously into what are called *operations*. Operations can be used on their own or queued up and prioritized to run asynchronously.

Operations are discussed more in depth in "Concurrency" on page 140, but let's look at how you can create a queue and add operations to it. To do this, we will use the NSOperationQueue class and NSOperation.

Because the NSOperation class is an abstract class, we will need to create a subclass to define our custom operation and add it to a queue:

```
framework 'Foundation'

class MyOperation < NSOperation
  attr_reader :name

  def initWithName(name)
    init
    @name = name
    self
  end

  def main
    puts "#{name} get to work!"
  end

end

operation_matt  = MyOperation.alloc.initWithName('Matt')

queue = NSOperationQueue.alloc.init
queue.addOperation(operation_matt)

# run the main loop for 2 seconds
NSRunLoop.currentRunLoop.runUntilDate(NSDate.dateWithTimeIntervalSinceNow(2.0))
```

To create a valid NSOperation subclass, we need to create a custom initiator (in this case, we used initWithName) and define a main method that will be executed when the operation is triggered.

 When creating a custom initiator, don't forget to return self.

Notifications

Most applications trigger a lot of events in the runtime, ranging from a user clicking on a UI element to an I/O operation. Cocoa's Foundation supplies a programming architecture that allows you to send and receive notifications and to subscribe to occurring events.

The notification architecture is divided into three parts: the notifications themselves, the notification centers, and the notification observers. When an event happens, a notification is created and sent to a notification center, which then broadcasts the notification to all the observers that registered for the event. Notifications can also be held in a notification queue before being broadcast.

NSNotification objects encapsulate information about events. The objects don't know much about anything except the event that sends them.

Notification Centers

If you need to manage notifications in just one process, use the NSNotificationCenter class. Otherwise, you will have to rely on NSDistributedNotificationCenter.

As explained earlier, notification centers receive notifications posted by events and dispatch them to registered observers. Observers are added to notification centers, and notifications can be manually posted to a center or automatically triggered by classes triggering notifications. The default notification center can be accessed using the NSNotificationCenter.defaultCenter method:

```
framework 'Foundation'

class NotificationHandler
  def tea_time(notification)
    puts "it's tea time!"
  end
end

center = NSNotificationCenter.defaultCenter
notification_handler = NotificationHandler.new

center.addObserver( notification_handler,
                    selector: "tea_time:",
                    name: 'tea_time_reminder',
                    object: nil )

center.postNotificationName("tea_time_reminder", object:self)
```

 A common problem reported by programmers new to notification centers is that their notifications are not working. This is often because their observers are garbage-collected, and, therefore, never get triggered. By design, observers use weak references instead of strong references, and registrations are automatically cleaned up when an observer is collected. You therefore need to ensure that the observers don't get garbage-collected for as long as you want the notification registration to remain. One way to do this is to assign them to instance variables of the class.

Notification Queues

One potential problem with notifications is that they are synchronous. Therefore, if an observer calls a slow method, the execution of the rest of the code is delayed. Notification queues, on the other hand, allow the coalescing of notifications as well as asynchronous posting.

As mentioned earlier, every thread has its own default notification center, but what I did not mention is that every default notification center also has a default notification queue. You can also create your own notification queue and associate it with a notification center.

To retrieve the default notification queue in the current thread, use the `defaultQueue` class method on `NSNotificationQueue`:

```
framework 'Foundation'
NSNotificationQueue.defaultQueue
# => #<NSNotificationQueue:0x200211100>
```

Now that you have a queue, you can post notifications to it. You have three options for doing this:

- Posting as soon as possible, bypassing the queue (but posting only at the end of current run loop iteration).
- Posting when the queue is idle.
- Posting synchronously but with coalescence. The notification queue coalesces (combines) messages in two ways: by discarding identical duplicates of a message that arrive during a given time period and by combining small messages into a single notification.

These notification styles or priorities are flags that you set when posting the notification. To dispatch a notification using each of the three priorities, retrieve the default notification queue for the current thread and create a notification that is ready to be posted:

```
framework 'Foundation'
queue = NSNotificationQueue.defaultQueue
notification = NSNotification.notificationWithName('fetch_feed', object:nil)
```

To post a notification as soon as possible, use the `NSPostASAP` style:

```
queue.enqueueNotification(notification, postingStyle: NSPostASAP)
```

This is often used for posting to an expensive resource, such as the display server, to avoid having many clients flushing the window buffer after drawing within the same run loop iteration. You can have all the clients post the same `NSPostASAP` style notification with coalescing on name and object. As a result, only one of those notifications is dispatched at the end of the run loop and the window buffer is flushed only once.

To post a notification when the run loop is waiting (idle), use the following:

```
queue.enqueueNotification(notification, postingStyle: NSPostWhenIdle)
```

Here is a simple example: imagine you are writing a text editor and you want to display some statistics at the bottom of the page, such as the number of lines, characters, words, and paragraphs in the buffer. If you were to recalculate this information every time a key is pressed, it would result in quite a lot of resource usage, especially if the user types quickly. Instead, you can queue the notifications using the `NSPostWhenIdle` style and post the information only when there is a pause in typing. This saves loads of resources.

The notification posting code will look like the following code. Imagine that `text_field` returns the main editor window with the text field we want to monitor:

```
notification = NSNotification.notificationWithName('text_edited', object:text_field)
queue = NSNotificationQueue.defaultQueue
queue.enqueueNotification(notification,
                          postingStyle: NSPostWhenIdle
                          coalesceMask: NSNotificationCoalescingOnName
                          forModes: nil)
```

The `coalesceMask` parameter tells the notification queue how to coalesce notifications. Notifications can be coalesced by name (`NSNotificationCoalescingOnName`) or by object (`NSNotificationCoalescingOnSender`). Alternatively, this parameter can disable coalescing (`NSNotificationNoCoalescing`). You can also combine the constants using the bitwise OR operator:

```
NSNotificationCoalescingOnSender | NSNotificationCoalescingOnName
```

Finally, to post a notification synchronously but still using the coalescence feature of the queue, use the following:

```
queue.enqueueNotification(notification, postingStyle: NSPostNow)
```

Using the `NSPostNow` style is the same thing as using `postNotification` or `notification WithName`, but it has the advantage of being able to combine similar notifications using coalescence. You will often want to use this type of notification when you want a synchronous behavior, basically, whenever you want to ensure that observing objects have received and processed the notification before doing something else. Using coalescence, you still ensure dispatched notifications are handled synchronously, but you also guarantee the uniqueness of these notifications.

Archiving and Serialization

There are situations where you need to convert some of your objects into a form that can be saved to a file or transmitted to another process or machine, and then reconstructed. The native binary format that represents objects in memory while you manipulate them is not appropriate for storage and may not be readable on another system. Therefore, Cocoa and Ruby provide standard ways to translate between the binary formats and a format more suitable for storage, often in a human-readable text format. Translating the data into such a format is known as *serialization* or *marshaling*.

In some cases, you just need to serialize a simple hierarchical relationship like an API response, whereas in other cases you need to archive complex relationships, as Interface Builder does when it stores the objects and relationships that make up a UI in a nib file.

In Cocoa, archiving uses the `NSCoder` abstract class, which can encode and decode Objective-C objects, scalars, arrays, structures, and strings. To be properly encoded and decoded, objects have to implement the `NSCoding` protocol. This defines two methods: one to encode the object and one to restore it. All of the `Foundation` primitive classes (NSString, NSArray, NSNumber, and so on) and most of the Application Kit UI objects implement the NSCoding protocol and can be put into an archive.

NSCoder has three types of archives, which differ in the encoding/decoding process they use:

Sequential archives
> Decoding is done in the same sequence in which the encoding took place. Use for sequential archives when your content needs to be processed linearly.

Keyed archives
> Information is encoded and decoded in a random access manner using assigned name keys. Because the keys can be requested by name, you can decode parts of the data in any order. This option offers flexibility for making serialized objects forward and backward compatible.

Distributed objects
> Used to implement distributed object architectures. To be used only when implementing distributed object architectures, which means when you want to do interprocess messaging between applications or threads.

Here is a simple keyed archiving process:

```
framework 'Foundation'
# let's assume we have a collection of Objective-C objects stored in
# a variable called objc_objects
archive_path = NSTemporaryDirectory().stringByAppendingPathComponent("Objs.archive")
result = NSKeyedArchiver.archiveRootObject( objc_objects, toFile: archive_path)
```

In Ruby, archiving is done using the Marshal class. All Ruby objects can be converted into a byte stream and then restored:

```
class CylonCenturion
  attr_accessor :battery_life, :ammo
end

class CylonSkinJob
  attr_accessor :physical_health, :mental_health
end
squadron = []
10.times{ squadron << CylonCenturion.new }
2.times{ squadron << CylonSkinJob.new }

# encode and save to file
File.open('cylon_squadron', 'w+'){|f| f << Marshal.dump(squadron)}
# reload
loaded_squadron = Marshal.load File.read('cylon_squadron')
leader = loaded_squadron.find{|soldier| soldier.is_a?(CylonSkinJob)}
```

Often, you don't need to serialize complex relationships and objects. What you need is to serialize some basic object types, such as to save some user's preferences to disk. To do that, you have a few options:

- writeToURL/writeToFile
- NSPropertyListSerialization
- YAML
- JSON

The `writeToURL/writeToFile` options were covered when we looked at the primitive classes added by `Foundation`. Refer to their documentation to see how to use this API:

For `NSPropertyListSerialization`, use the following:

```
framework 'Foundation'
user_info = { :points       => 4200,
              :level        => 3,
              :name         => 'Matt',
              :teams        => ['Blue', 'Red'],
              :twitter_update => false,
              :urls         => {:github  => 'http://github.com/mattetti',
                                :twitter => 'http://twitter.com/merbist'}
            }

plist_data = NSPropertyListSerialization.dataWithPropertyList(
                                          user_info,
                                          format: NSPropertyListXMLFormat_v1_0,
                                          options: 0,
                                          error: nil)

file_path = NSTemporaryDirectory().stringByAppendingPathComponent("user_info.plist")
plist_data.writeToFile(file_path, atomically:true)
```

You can also use MacRuby's syntactical sugar:

```
user_info = { :points       => 4200,
              :level        => 3,
              :name         => 'Matt',
              :teams        => ['Blue', 'Red'],
              :twitter_update => false,
              :urls         => {:github  => 'http://github.com/mattetti',
                                :twitter => 'http://twitter.com/merbist'}
            }
plist = user_info.to_plist
```

Here is what the file content looks like:

```
<?xml version="1.0" encoding="UTF-8"?>
<!DOCTYPE plist PUBLIC "-//Apple//DTD PLIST 1.0//EN"
"http://www.apple.com/DTDs/PropertyList-1.0.dtd">
<plist version="1.0">
<dict>
        <key>level</key>
        <integer>3</integer>
        <key>name</key>
        <string>Matt</string>
        <key>points</key>
        <integer>4200</integer>
        <key>teams</key>
```

```
<array>
        <string>Blue</string>
        <string>Red</string>
</array>
<key>twitter_update</key>
<false/>
<key>urls</key>
<dict>
        <key>github</key>
        <string>http://github.com/mattetti</string>
        <key>twitter</key>
        <string>http://twitter.com/merbist</string>
</dict>
</dict>
</plist>
```

To load and recover the object, you can reload the object and use the following code:

```
framework 'Foundation'
file_path = File.expand_path("~/user_info.plist")
plist_data = NSData.alloc.initWithContentsOfFile(file_path)
user_info = NSPropertyListSerialization.propertyListFromData(plist_data,
                                    mutabilityOption:
        NSPropertyListMutableContainersAndLeaves,
                                    format:nil,
                                    errorDescription:nil)

p user_info
# => {"points"=>4200, "twitter_update"=>false,
"urls"=>{"github"=>"http://github.com/mattetti",
 "twitter"=>"http://twitter.com/merbist"}, "level"=>3,
"teams"=>["Blue", "Red"], "name"=>"Matt"}
```

Notice that in this example, I chose to use the plist XML format, but I could have chosen to use the plist binary format instead.

Another way to deserialize a property list file is to use MacRuby's helper to convert the content of the plist file:

```
file_path = File.expand_path("~/user_info.plist")
user_info = load_plist(File.read(file_path))
```

Because we know the type of object we are expecting from the deserialization (a dictionary), we could have also done the following:

```
file_path = File.expand_path("~/user_info.plist")
Hash.dictionaryWithContentsOfFile(file_path)
```

To encode basic types, we can also use YAML or JSON:

```
require 'yaml'
user_info = {"points"=>4200, "twitter_update"=>false, "urls"=>{"github"=>
 "http://github.com/mattetti", "twitter"=>"http://twitter.com/merbist"}, "level"=>3,
 "teams"=>["Blue", "Red"], "name"=>"Matt"}
File.open('user_info.yml', 'w+'){|f| f << user_info.to_yaml}
```

The content of the YAML file looks like the following:

```
---
points: 4200
twitter_update: false
urls:
  github: http://github.com/mattetti
  twitter: http://twitter.com/merbist
level: 3
teams:
- Blue
- Red
name: Matt
```

To deserialize the content of the file, simply do the following:

```
require 'yaml'
YAML.load_file('user_info.yml')
# => {"points"=>4200, "name"=>"Matt", "twitter_update"=>false,
"urls"=>{"twitter"=>"http://twitter.com/merbist", "github"=>
"http://github.com/mattetti"}, "level"=>3, "teams"=>["Blue", "Red"]}
```

Finally, you can use the JSON serialization format, as follows:

```
require 'json'
user_info = {"points"=>4200, "twitter_update"=>false, "urls"=>{"github"=>
"http://github.com/mattetti", "twitter"=>"http://twitter.com/merbist"}, "level"=>3,
 "teams"=>["Blue", "Red"], "name"=>"Matt"}
File.open('user_info.json', 'w+'){|f| f << user_info.to_json}
```

The content of the saved file looks like this:

```
{"points":4200,"name":"Matt","twitter_update":false,
 "urls":{"twitter":"http://twitter.com/merbist",
 "github":"http://github.com/mattetti"},"level":3,"teams":["Blue","Red"]}
```

To deserialize the file, use `JSON.load`:

```
require 'json'
JSON.parse File.open('user_info.json').read
# => {"points"=>4200, "teams"=>["Blue", "Red"], "twitter_update"=>false,
 "name"=>"Matt", "urls"=>{"twitter"=>"http://twitter.com/merbist",
 "github"=>"http://github.com/mattetti"}, "level"=>3}
```

Miscellaneous Classes

The `Foundation` framework also comes with other useful miscellaneous classes.

XML Parsing

Foundation offers two approaches to XML parsing: an event-driven parser called `NSXMLParser` and a `NSXMLNode` based solution using XPath.

The `NSXMLParser` solution is useful for processing a complete XML file, and is based on delegates. You need to initiate an `NSXMLParser` object with a URL or data. In the following example, I use `NSXMLParser.alloc.initWithContentsOfURL` to load XML from a

URL. I then specify a delegate that will be called when the parser finds elements. Once that is done, I call **parse** on the parser object.

Here is a Really Simple Syndication parser built using **NSXMLParser**. I won't go through the details of this script, but the overall structure gives you an idea of how this kind of parser works. There is documentation for NSXMLParser delegates (*http://developer .apple.com/mac/library/documentation/cocoa/reference/NSXMLParserDelegate_Proto col/Reference/Reference.html*) at the Apple developer site:

```ruby
framework 'Cocoa'
class RSSParser
  attr_accessor :parser, :xml_url, :doc

  def initialize(xml_url)
    @xml_url = xml_url
    NSApplication.sharedApplication
    url = NSURL.alloc.initWithString(xml_url)
    @parser = NSXMLParser.alloc.initWithContentsOfURL(url)
    @parser.shouldProcessNamespaces = true
    @parser.delegate = self
    @items = []
  end

  # RSSItem is a simple class that holds all of the RSS items.
  # Extend this class to display/process the item differently.
  class RSSItem
    attr_accessor :title, :description, :link, :guid, :pubDate, :enclosure
    def initialize
      @title, @description, @link, @pubDate, @guid = '', '', '', '', ''
    end
  end

  # Starts the parsing and send each parsed item through its block.
  #
  # Usage:
  #    feed.block_while_parsing do |item|
  #       puts item.link
  #    end
  def parse(&block)
    @block = block
    puts "Parsing #{xml_url}"
    @parser.parse
  end

  # Starts the parsing but keeps blocking the main run loop
  # until the parsing is done.
  # Do not use this method in a GUI app. Use #parse instead.
  def block_while_parsing(&block)
    @parsed = false
    parse(&block)
    NSRunLoop.currentRunLoop.runUntilDate(NSDate.distantFuture)
  end

  # Delegate getting called when parsing starts
```

```ruby
def parserDidStartDocument(parser)
  puts "starting parsing.."
end

# Delegate being called when an element starts being processed
def parser(parser, didStartElement:element, namespaceURI:uri, qualifiedName:name,
                                                              attributes:attrs)
  if element == 'item'
    @current_item = RSSItem.new
  elsif element == 'enclosure'
    @current_item.enclosure = attrs
  end
  @current_element = element
end

# as the parser finds characters, this method is being called
def parser(parser, foundCharacters:string)
  if @current_item && @current_item.respond_to?(@current_element)
    el = @current_item.send(@current_element)
    el << string
  end
end

# method called when an element is done being parsed
def parser(parser, didEndElement:element, namespaceURI:uri, qualifiedName:name)
  if element == 'item'
    @items << @current_item
  end
end

# delegate getting called when the parsing is done
# If a block was set, it will be called on each parsed item
def parserDidEndDocument(parser)
  @parsed = true
  puts "done parsing"
  if @block
    @items.each{|item| @block.call(item)}
  end
end

end

twitter = RSSParser.new("http://twitter.com/statuses/user_timeline/16476741.rss")

# because we are running in a script, we need the run loop to keep running
# until we are done with parsing
#
# If we would to use the above code in a GUI app,
# we would use #parse instead of #block_while_parsing
twitter.block_while_parsing do |item|
  print item.title
end
```

The delegate object should implement some methods so it is alerted when the parser encounters an event. Delegate methods look like the following:

```
def parser(parser, didStartElement:element, namespaceURI:uri, qualifiedName:name,
    attributes:attrs)
end
```

This method, for instance, is called when the parser encounters the beginning of an element. It's up to the developer to set up the proper business logic to capture and process the information that the parser outputs.

In some cases, however, you already know the structure of the XML document you are going to process and you will want to access just one or a limited set of notes. To do that, you can rely on NSXMLNode/NSXMLDocument and XPath or XQuery.

Here is a simple example that fetches the MacRuby home page and searches for the current version using XPath:

```
framework 'Foundation'
url = NSURL.alloc.initWithString('http://macruby.org')
url_content = NSMutableString.alloc.initWithContentsOfURL(url,
                                        encoding:NSUTF8StringEncoding,
                                        error:nil)
data = url_content.dataUsingEncoding(NSUTF8StringEncoding)
document = NSXMLDocument.alloc.initWithData(data, options:NSXMLDocumentTidyHTML,
                                        error:nil)
root = document.rootElement
version_xpath = '//*[@id="current_version"]'
error = Pointer.new(:object)
nodes = root.nodesForXPath(version_xpath, error:error)
if nodes.empty?
  puts error[0].description
else
  puts nodes.first.stringValue
end
```

Filtering/Logical Conditions

Using Ruby's enumerators and blocks, you can query a collection of objects. The following example illustrates the procedure:

```
Actor = Struct.new :name, :oscars
actors = []
actors << Actor.new("Marlon Brando", 2)
actors << Actor.new("Sean Penn", 2)
actors << Actor.new("Jack Nicholson", 3)
actors << Actor.new("Adrien Brody", 1)
actors << Actor.new("Neil Patrick Harris", 0)

winners = actors.find_all{|actor| actor.oscars >= 1 }
# => [#<struct Actor name="Marlon Brando", oscars=2>, #<struct Actor name="Sean Penn",
   oscars=2>, #<struct Actor name="Jack Nicholson", oscars=3>,
#<struct Actor name="Adrien Brody", oscars=1>]

max_oscars = actors.map{|actor| actor.oscars}.max
super_star = winners.find{|actor| actor.oscars == max_oscars}
# => #<struct Actor name="Marlon Brando", oscars=3>
```

The code within curly braces resembles what you would put in a **do** loop. The first enumerator, for instance, is:

```
|actor| actor.oscars >= 1
```

Ruby mixes in the `Enumerable` module in collection classes to offer various traversal and searching methods such as `max`, `find`, and `find_all`. Thus, as part of the `find_all` method, the previous code extracts each item that is associated with one or more Oscar awards.

 In this example, I did not explicitly create the `Actor` class and its accessors. Instead, I used the `Struct` class to generate the `Actor` class. Read the Ruby documentation to learn more about this interesting way to generate simple classes.

In Cocoa, filtering and searching uses the `NSPredicate` class. As the Cocoa documentation explains quite well, this class is used to define logical conditions that constrain a search either for a fetch or for in-memory filtering. However, `NSPredicate` can be used only on objects that implement the key-value coding (KVC) protocol, which can be done manually on custom objects.

Here are a few examples using `NSPredicate`:

```
framework 'Foundation'
predicate = NSPredicate.predicateWithFormat("SELF IN %@", ['Ninh', 'Hongli'])
predicate.evaluateWithObject "Matt"
# => false

filter = NSPredicate.predicateWithFormat("SELF beginswith[c] 'm'")
['Matt', 'Mike', 'Nate'].filteredArrayUsingPredicate(filter)
# => ["Matt", "Mike"]
```

Undo/Redo

Undo and redo are common patterns in applications that revert the state of an object. Before the user changes the state of an object, the object registers the initial state as well as the method called on the object. This way, the change can be undone and redone.

The `NSUndoManager` class is implemented in the `Foundation` framework because executables other than applications might want to revert changes to their states.

Application Kit also implements undo and redo in its `NSTextView` class, making it available to all its subclasses.

Here is an example implementing undo/redo on a player class:

```
framework 'Foundation'

class Player
```

```
      attr_accessor :x, :y

      def initialize
        @x = @y = 0
      end

      def undo_manager
        @manager ||= NSUndoManager.alloc.init
      end

      def left
        undo_manager.prepareWithInvocationTarget(self).right
        @x -= 1
      end

      def right
        undo_manager.prepareWithInvocationTarget(self).left
        @x += 1
      end
    end
```

And now if we used the code, here is what it would look like:

```
>> lara = Player.new
=> <Player:0x200267c80 @y=0 @x=0>
>> lara.undo_manager.canUndo
=> false # normal since we did not do anything yet
>> lara.left
=> -1
>> lara.x # -1
=> -1
>> lara.undo_manager.canUndo
=> true # now we can undo, so let's try
>> lara.undo_manager.undo # undo back to initial position
=> #<NSUndoManager:0x200257560>
>> lara.x
=> 0
>> lara.undo_manager.canUndo
=> false # we can't do any more undoing
>> lara.undo_manager.canRedo
=> true # however i can redo what was just undone
>> lara.undo_manager.redo # redo to before we called undo
=> #<NSUndoManager:0x200257560>
>> lara.x
=> -1
```

User's Preferences

Foundation offers a convenient way to store a user's preferences via the NSUserDe
faults class. Preferences are saved in a shared database where developers can save and
load keyed settings using some primitive objects. Here is a quick example that saves a
token in the user's preferences. Keep on reading after the example to see how to save
other object types, such as arrays and hashes, and search for a preference key:

```
framework 'Foundation'

def set_api_token(token)
  NSUserDefaults.standardUserDefaults['oreilly.api_token'] = token
  NSUserDefaults.standardUserDefaults.synchronize # force sync
  api_token
end

def api_token
  NSUserDefaults.standardUserDefaults["oreilly.api_token"]
end

if api_token.nil?
  puts "The API token has not been set yet, please enter it now:"
  cli_token = gets
  set_api_token(cli_token.strip)
  puts "API token set, thank you!"
else
  puts "Currently stored API token: #{api_token}"
end
```

After saving this code in a file called *api_pref.rb*, run it from the command line. The output will look like the following:

```
$ macruby api_pref.rb
The API token has not been set yet, please enter it now:
# typed my token: 42sosayweall42
API token set, thank you!
```

Running it a second time will skip the token prompt:

```
$ macruby api_pref.rb
Currently stored API token: 42sosayweall42
```

Let's jump to *macirb* and play with the preferences:

```
$ macirb --simple-prompt
>> require 'api_pref.rb'
Currently stored API token: 42sosayweall42
=> true
>> NSUserDefaults.standardUserDefaults.removeObjectForKey('oreilly.api_token')
=> #<NSUserDefaults:0x2002362a0>
>> api_token
=> nil
>> set_api_token 'macruby is awesome'
=> "macruby is awesome"
>> api_token
=> "macruby is awesome"
>> NSUserDefaults.standardUserDefaults.dictionaryRepresentation.keys.grep /oreilly/
-> ["oreilly.api_token"]
>> NSUserDefaults.standardUserDefaults['oreilly.owned_books'] =
[{'topic' => 'macruby',
  'isbn' => '9781449380373'}]
>> NSUserDefaults.standardUserDefaults['oreilly.owned_books'].first['isbn']
=> "9781449380373"
```

As shown here, we can delete preferences using `NSUserDefaults.stand`
`ardUserDefaults.removeObjectForKey`, as well as access all the preferences using `NSUserDefaults.standardUserDefaults.dictionaryRepresenta`
`tion`, which returns a `Hash`.

Finally, we set a more complex preference: an array containing a hash. However, the
storage is limited to objects supported by the property lists, that is, objects of the following class families: `NSData`, `NSString`, `NSNumber`, `NSDate`, `NSArray`, and `NSDictionary`.

## CHAPTER 5

Application Kit

The Application Kit, also known as the `AppKit` framework, contains all the classes needed to build OS X GUI applications. This is the framework we used in our "Hello World!" example in "Code Example" on page 7.

`AppKit` is a very large framework and this book will not cover all the classes provided. I'll introduce the concepts you need to get started and illustrate a few of the classes that every programmer uses for graphical interfaces.

Cocoa Key Principles

You need to understand a few key concepts before digging further into Cocoa. So far, we have looked closely only at the `Foundation` classes, which map fairly intuitively to concepts and library calls in other programming languages and programming environments. With Cocoa, we jump into unique concepts that are less intuitive.

Cocoa is a well-thought-out, well-designed, and very consistent API. To assure this consistency, a few key concepts underlie most of the API classes. By following the designed conventions, you will avoid spending a lot of time rewriting your code over and over.

 These Cocoa concepts and conventions are unfortunately not enforced in all the available frameworks. Some C-based frameworks were incorporated into Cocoa simply by adding an Objective-C wrapper, and these usually don't follow the conventions as nicely as frameworks written directly in Objective-C.

Model-View-Controller Design Pattern

Ruby developers who have done any web development should be quite familiar with the model-view-controller (MVC) design pattern. It's one of the key conventions enforced by the Ruby on Rails framework, and it goes back to the early 1980s when the

Smalltalk community defined it, so it can also be found in plenty of other environments: GTK, Tcl Tk, Qt, Swing, WPF, and many others, including Cocoa. Basically, your code ends up divided in three parts: the *model*, which represents the data upon which the application operates, the *view*, which renders the model and potentially makes it interactive, and finally the *controller*, which is the glue between the model and the view and runs what many people call the "business logic" unique to your application.

When developing a Cocoa app, you will usually define your views in *Interface Builder*, Cocoa's UI tool, while your models and controllers will be written in your editor/IDE (usually *Xcode*). We will go through these tools later in this chapter.

Protocols

As you have probably guessed, a Cocoa protocol has nothing to do with the international agreement aimed at ending child labor in the production of cocoa, known as the *Cocoa Protocol* and signed in September 2001.

Protocols are well-defined APIs that any class may choose to implement. In other words, protocols are a way to declare a convention via an API. Two classes implementing the same protocol can easily communicate with each other without having to be subclasses of the same superclass.

Protocols are basically just a set of well-defined methods adopted by different classes. Some APIs expect to receive certain objects to implement certain protocols. So if you are developing your own class, you will need to make sure to implement the expected API. Once you do, we say that your class *conforms* to the protocol.

Key-Value Coding

Often abbreviated KVC, the NSKeyValueCoding protocol defines the mechanism to set and retrieve an object's attributes/properties by name instead of by invoking a method. This is a fundamental value concept in Cocoa programming, and it essentially allows you to access instances as if they were hash tables/dictionaries. There are many advantages of such an approach. The most obvious are that you don't need to explicitly write getters and setters and that you can implement UI bindings and serialization much more easily, since knowing the name of a property is enough to get and set it.

 KVC is often mentioned with KVO (key value observing), which is a notification system using the observer pattern and based on KVC.

Here is a simple example in which we will pretend that Player is a KVC-compliant class:

```
matt = Player.new

matt.setPoints(42)
matt.valueForKey('points') # => 42
matt.setValue(442, forKey: 'points')
matt.valueForKey('points') # => 442
```

The Player class doesn't have to implement a setPoints accessor method. Because the class implements the NSKeyValueCoding protocol, it intercepts your invocation of set Points and sets the points instance variable in your instance to the value you supply. The other three methods shown here are also interpreted according to the protocol.

The code you can write using this protocol is quite similar to Ruby's accessor syntax:

```
matt = Player.new

matt.points = 42
matt.points # => 42
matt.points = 442
matt.points # => 442
```

You can simply implement it like this:

```
class Player
  attr_accessor :points
end
```

It turns out that MacRuby generates the KVC code for you when you add a Ruby accessor. This way, your classes can easily conform to the KVC protocol:

```
framework 'foundation'
class Player
  attr_accessor :points
end

matt = Player.new
matt.points = 100 # Ruby syntax
matt.valueForKey('points') # => 100 (KVC protocol)
matt.setPoints(42) # KVC protocol
matt.points # => 42
matt.setValue(442, forKey: 'points') # KVC protocol
matt.points # => 442
```

Here is another example using a class that's KVC-compliant by default: Hash and a KVC method named valueForKeyPath that we haven't seen yet:

```
framework "Cocoa"
class Me < Hash
  def initialize
    super
    self["siblings"] = {"brothers" => ["Arnaud"], "sister" => ["Marjorie"]}
  end
end

moi = Me.new
p moi.valueForKey('siblings')
```

```
# => {"brothers"=>["Arnaud"], "sister"=>["Marjorie"]}
p moi.valueForKeyPath("siblings.brothers")
# => ["Arnaud"]
```

In this example, we create a new class called Me that inherits from Hash and therefore is KVC-compliant by default. We define the initialize method to set some default value. The method starts by calling super so the code defined by the Hash constructor can be triggered, then sets the default values. Once my code is written, we create an instance of Me called moi and use the previously discussed valueForKey method, which works as expected. Then we invoke another KVC protocol method, called valueForKeyPath, which takes a path to the object we are interested in. Notice that valueForKeyPath requires a scalar as its argument; we can't pass it an array index. For instance, passing **siblings.brothers[0]** will result in a nil value.

Bindings

When developing a Cocoa application, you can bind an attribute of one object to a property of another. For instance, imagine we are developing a music player. On the one hand, we have a player object defining a volume attribute, and on the other, we have a slider UI controller to allow the user to control the output volume. We also want to display the setting of the volume. To implement all this, we are going to load our player instance in the controller and bind its volume attribute to our slider and text field values.

Let's start by defining our model. Create a new Xcode MacRuby project (see the intro to Xcode to learn more about Xcode) and add a new Ruby file called *player.rb*. Our model code is very simple—just a KVC conform class with a volume attribute, as shown here:

```
class Player
  attr_accessor :volume
end
```

Our AppDelegate class is not much more complicated, we just need to add a new accessor for the player and initialize an instance of the object when the class instance is initialized:

```
class AppDelegate
  attr_accessor :window
  attr_accessor :player

  def applicationDidFinishLaunching(a_notification)
    # Insert code here to initialize your application
  end

  def initialize
    @player = Player.new
  end

end
```

Now edit your view file (*MainMenu.xib*) by clicking on it in Xcode.

The template already has an `NSObject` instance called *App Delegate*, which represents an instance of the `AppDelegate` class (Figure 5-1). Look at it via the Identity Inspector and notice that the `AppDelegate` class is set as the object's class.

Figure 5-1. Details of the controller object viewed in the Inspector

Now open the Object Library, look for the vertical slider, drop it on the UI inside the window's view (Figure 5-2), then look for the text field icon and drop it inside the view, as shown in Figure 5-3.

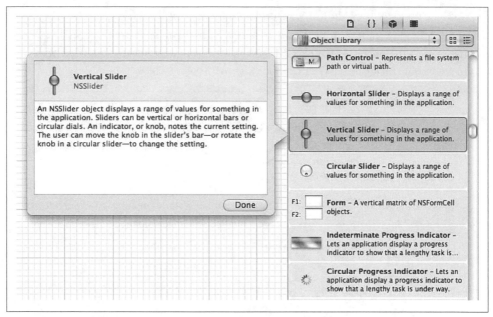

Figure 5-2. Vertical slider viewed from the Object Library

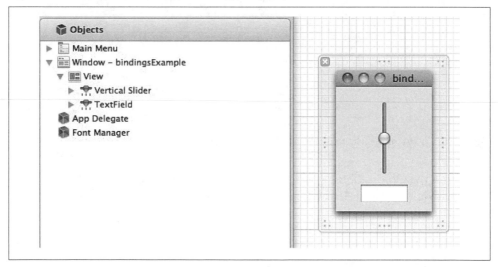

Figure 5-3. Object hierarchy and UI

Once the UI objects are in place, you need to set the bindings for the slider. To do so, select the slider and open it in the Inspector. Then select the bindings tab in the Utility area and set the bindings settings as shown in Figure 5-4.

Set the bind to `App Delegate` and set the model key path to `player.volume`. Do the same for the text field. The slider will set the value while the text field will read the value.

Figure 5-4. Slider's bindings viewed in the Inspector

Save your project and run the app from Xcode by clicking the Run button or by using the Command + R shortcut. The end result should look something like Figure 5-5.

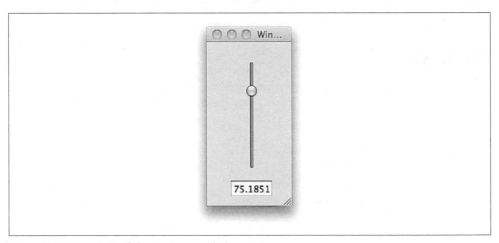

Figure 5-5. View of the slider in the compiled app

When you move the slider, the text value changes, and vice versa. But, what's even more interesting is that the model's attribute value also changes at the same time. As you can see, bindings can save you a lot of development time.

Delegation

We used and discussed delegation when we worked on our "Hello World!" example in Chapter 1. In the delegate class we created, we implemented two delegate methods. One was an `NSApplication` delegate named `applicationDidFinishLaunching` and the other was an `NSWindow` delegate named `windowWillClose`.

Delegation is a common pattern in Cocoa. It often offers an elegant way to hook into events. For instance, when an application is started, two delegates are triggered if they are available. The `applicationWillFinishLaunching` delegate is called as soon as the run loop is ready, but before the application is started. `applicationDidFinishLaunching` is called after the application is launched.

An `NSWindow` instance has a lot of delegates available for implementation (see *http://developer.apple.com/mac/library/documentation/cocoa/reference/NSWindowDelegate_Protocol/Reference/Reference.html*). A few of the simpler delegates include:

- `windowShouldClose`
- `windowWillClose`
- `windowWillMove`
- `windowDidMove`

Look at the documentation to learn more about the delegates available for the classes you are using.

User Interface

Most of the UI-related classes are provided by the Cocoa framework. Instead of going down the long list of UI classes, let's talk about the main concepts and elements critical to MacRuby developers.

Windows, Views, and Cells

Windows, views, and cells are the visible units the user deals with. For instance, a button is usually a view, as is a text entry box.

Windows and panels

Windows are conceptually easy to understand and don't need much explanation. Technically, a Cocoa window is an instance of the `NSWindow` class in which a view

(`NSView` instance) displays its content. To group windows, an application can use panels via the `NSPanel` class, which is itself a subclass of `NSWindow`.

Views

Per Cocoa's definition, "A view instance is responsible for drawing and responding to user actions in a rectangular region of a window." In other words, views render some of the app content and handle user-initiated events.

Whenever you need to display content in a window, you will need a view. The view also handles keyboard and mouse events. Views often act as containers and contain one or more nested views.

The primary view class is called `NSView`, which inherits directly from `NSResponder`. This lets you easily implement keyboard/mouse event handling by overriding `NSView` methods. This class implements the fundamental view behavior, making it a perfect candidate for creating a custom view.

Application Kit offers a set of great `NSView` subclasses to help with common tasks. Here are a few examples:

- Controls such as buttons via `NSButton`
- Text fields and display via `NSTextField` and `NSTextView`
- PDF display via `PDFView`
- Movie display via `QTMovieView`
- Image display via `NSImageView`
- Open GL contexts via `NSOpenGLView`

Cells

For reasons of performance and reusability, most views delegate drawing to another class called the *cell* (generally an `NSCell` subclass). For instance, buttons are instances of the `NSButton` class (itself a subclass of `NSControl`), but use different `NSButtonCell` instances for drawing.

Positioning

The position of an object is called its *coordinates*, and this refers to the x and y pixel positions of its bottom, leftmost corner. When using Cocoa views, it's important to keep in mind that the coordinates of each object are always relative to the immediately enclosing view. Thus, each of the views you create will define and maintain its own coordinate systems. All the objects in each view will be relative to the view's coordinate system.

By default, as shown in Figure 5-6, the origin is at (`0.0, 0.0`), which is located in the lower left corner of the parent object.

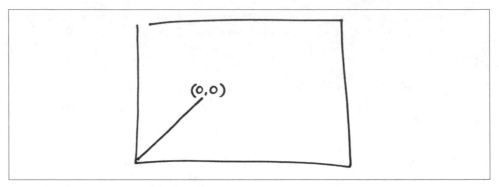

Figure 5-6. Representation of the drawing origin

Let's take an example. Imagine that we want to display a web page in a window. The web page's view should take up only a quarter of the window and we want it to be at the top left corner (Figure 5-7).

Figure 5-7. Window with a web preview on top left corner

You could just use Interface Builder to create such a simple UI, but for the sake of explaining how views work, I will show how to programmatically create a window and content view, and to place a web page view on the top left corner of the window. Here is the code:

```
framework 'Cocoa'
framework 'WebKit'

application = NSApplication.sharedApplication

# create the window
width  = 800.0
height = 600.0
frame  = [0.0, 0.0, width, height]
mask = NSTitledWindowMask | NSClosableWindowMask | NSMiniaturizableWindowMask
window = NSWindow.alloc.initWithContentRect(frame,
          styleMask:mask,
          backing:NSBackingStoreBuffered,
```

```
                defer:false)

    # assign a content view instance
    content_view = NSView.alloc.initWithFrame(frame)
    window.contentView = content_view

    # create a web view positioned in the top left quarter of the super view
    web_view_frame = [0.0, height/2, width/2, height/2]
    web_view = WebView.alloc.initWithFrame(web_view_frame, frameName: "Web Frame",
    groupName: nil)
    request = NSURLRequest.requestWithURL(NSURL.URLWithString("http://macruby.org"))
    web_view.mainFrame.loadRequest(request)
    content_view.addSubview(web_view)

    # center the window
    window.center

    # show the window
    window.display
    window.makeKeyAndOrderFront(nil)
    window.orderFrontRegardless

    application.run
```

You can copy this code to a file and run it with the MacRuby executable. I will skip the part about requiring the frameworks and creating an application.

We start the code by creating a frame for our window:

```
    width  = 800.0
    height = 600.0
    frame  = [0.0, 0.0, width, height]
```

Technically, a frame is just an array with four floating-point values representing the x-axis coordinate, y-axis coordinate, width, and height. An Objective-C code example would have the following syntax:

```
    NSRect frame = NSMakeRect(0.0, 0.0, 800.0, 600.0);
```

Both code snippets just shown are equivalent, except that one is written in Ruby and the other in Objective-C.

A frame defines the size of its content and its position inside the containing views. A frame in Cocoa can be considered like a picture frame in real life: you position it on the wall and the frame dimensions define the maximum area available for the canvas inside.

Our example starts by creating a window that will hold our UI. We define two variables, width and height, that we use for the frame. We will reuse these variables later on to position our web page view relative to the window.

We also need to create a content view that will hold our UI items. Remember that we want our web page view to take only one-fourth of the space. For that to happen, we need a placeholder. That's what our NSView instance offers:

```
content_view = NSView.alloc.initWithFrame(frame)
window.contentView = content_view
```

 If you start a new Interface Builder Application project, a window and its content view instance will already be created for you.

Now we need to create a frame for our web view. This frame is positioned relative to the content view, which in turn is positioned relative to our window. Since we stored the window's width and height, we can easily define our web view frame to be displayed only at the top left corner of our GUI:

```
web_view_frame = [0.0, height/2, width/2, height/2]
```

Our frame defines the web view x-axis position as 0.0, which is the graphics environment axis origin and located all the way to the left. Then we do some math to define the y-axis position, width, and height. We take the superview (content_view) height and divide it in two to find the middle point to position our web view. Because we want our web view to only take a fourth of the UI, we set the width and the height to be half the corresponding width and the height of the containing view.

 Remember that we are starting to draw from the bottom left and not from the top, as you do when designing a web page.

We then create the WebView instance, set the URL to load, and finally add it to the content view subviews:

```
content_view.addSubview(web_view)
```

At this point, we are finished placing our content. However, why not center our window on the user's screen while we are at it?

```
window.center
```

Calling the center instance method on a window places it exactly in the center horizontally and somewhat above center vertically. Another way to center the window is to manually locate its frame:

```
screen_frame = NSScreen.mainScreen.frame
window.frameOrigin = [(screen_frame.size.width - width)/2.0,
                      ((screen_frame.size.height - height)/2.0)]
```

This code starts by retrieving the screen frame. Then we position our window right in the middle of the screen by taking the width and height of the screen, subtracting our UI width and height, and dividing the sum by 2.

On my laptop, my resolution is set to 1280x800. So, to find the x coordinate, our code takes the screen width (1280), subtracts our content view's width (800), and divides the result by 2, locating the x coordinate at 240.0. We do the same with the height and get a y coordinate of 100.0.

Once we have the coordinates figured out, we move the window frame origin and display the window.

Great, our content displays properly—but what if we want to track keyboard and/or mouse events?

Events and the Responder Chain

When an event message is dispatched, the message is sent down the window. The window itself has a responder chain, which is a linked series of responder objects. If the first object in the chain doesn't handle the message, the message is passed to the next responder in the chain and so forth, until a responder handles the message or the responder chain has been entirely traversed (in which case the window's responder noResponderFor method is dispatched).

 If you have multiple windows, only the window in which the associated user event occurred will forward the event message to its responder chain.

The default responder chain is constructed by the Application Kit framework, but can be modified by developers. The default responder chain for a key event begins with the first responder in the window where the focus is when the key is pressed. In contrast, the default responder chain for a mouse event begins with the view on which the event occurred. If not handled, the mouse event message is sent to the window's first responder, which is usually the selected view object. The next responder in the chain is the UI object's containing view (superview) and so on up to the NSWindow object.

You can insert responders in the responder chain by using the setNextResponder method or the nextResponder= alias on the view object.

Let's experiment with the responder chain. Open Xcode and create a new project using the MacRuby application template. Now create a new Ruby file and call it *event_view.rb*. Our new class will be a View subclass that will handle our events:

```ruby
class EventView < NSView

  def acceptsFirstResponder
    true
  end

  def keyDown(event)
    puts "key down"
```

```
      characters = event.characters
      if characters.length == 1 && !event.isARepeat
        character = characters.characterAtIndex(0)
          case character
          when NSLeftArrowFunctionKey
            puts "you pressed the left arrow"
           when NSRightArrowFunctionKey
            puts "you pressed the right arrow"
          end
        end
      end

    end
```

The subclass implements a keyDown method that takes an event argument. This method is part of the responder chain. You can see from the example that we can get the characters pressed by calling **characters** on the event. We inspect the characters pressed to log an appropriate message. We then check that the event isn't a repeated event, in the sense that if the user leaves his or her finger on a key, we want to get only one event. We extract the characters (**NSString** instance) from the event (**NSEvent**). We then take only the first character using **characterAtindex** and try to match it to some keyboard constants.

Now click on the *MainMenu.xib* file. The contents will be displayed in a format like that shown in Figure 5-8.

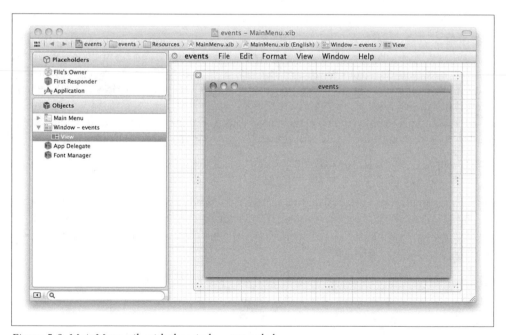

Figure 5-8. MainMenu.xib with the window expanded

Select the View in the Identity Inspector and, in the Custom Class section, change the class value to `EventView` (see Figure 5-9). Xcode automatically detects the new class we created.

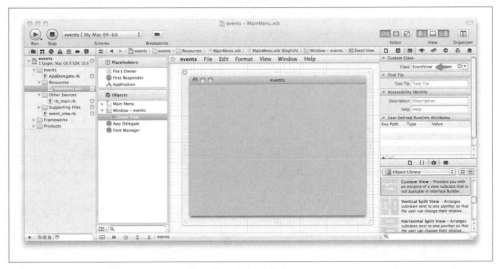

Figure 5-9. View with a custom class handling keystrokes

Save the project and click Run. When the application is running, type on your keyboard and see the output in the Debug area (shown in Figure 5-10). Try pressing the left or right arrow keys and notice the different output.

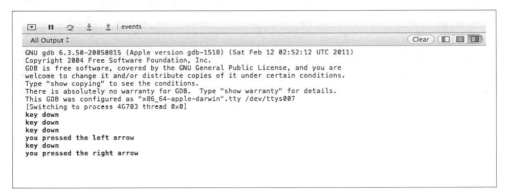

Figure 5-10. Output shown in the Debug area

To see which key events are available, read the `NSResponder` class documentation (*http://developer.apple.com/mac/library/documentation/cocoa/Reference/ApplicationKit/Classes/NSResponder_Class/Reference/Reference.html*). What we did was to set our custom view as first responder and check the key pressed to see whether it matched one of the `NSResponder`'s constants.

Drawing

Cocoa's drawing environment is available via the Application Kit framework, which is itself based on Quartz, the Macintosh's basic 2D graphics rendering software. The environment automatically takes advantage of graphics hardware wherever it can, making the drawing process as fast as possible.

If you come from a browser-oriented background, you might not think about how UI elements are rendered. After all, when using HTML, you just use UI tags and let the browser deal with rendering. In Cocoa, however, understanding how UI elements are drawn and how to interact with the drawing processing can be very beneficial. If you use only standard system controls, all the drawing is automatically handled by Cocoa. But as soon as you start using custom views and controls, managing the customized appearance of your elements become your responsibility. Also, you might want to use the drawing features to display images, PDFs, vector-based drawings, or videos, to render openGL code, or to custom print.

But before getting too deep into custom drawing, let's talk more about how a normal control element is drawn.

A control element such as a button is usually an instance of a custom `NSView` class. `NSView` instances are responsible for their own drawing, but in most views the drawing is delegated to another class called the cell (generally a subclass of `NSCell`).

In the case of `NSButton`, the drawing is delegated to an `NSButtonCell` instance. To customize the drawing of a button, you can subclass the cell and override some of its properties or methods. The advantage of having the drawing done in the cell instead of the view is that one cell instance can be shared by multiple controls of the same kind. Also, a cell can be given to a more specialized view to customize only a part of it. A good example of this is customizing a table view column using a different cell.

If you look at the Interface Builder library and search for `NSButton`, you will find a lot of different buttons (Figure 5-11). That's because each button uses a different `NSButtonCell` under the covers to implement its own UI. The `NSButtonCell` associated with the button will set the background color, style, images, states, sounds, and events. It will also take care of the button's content drawing.

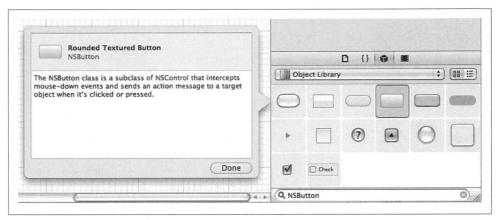

Figure 5-11. Choice of NSButton types offered by the Object Library

When the button is loaded, Cocoa draws it in its initial state. When a mouse event occurs on the button or a triggering key is pressed, the NSButtonCell state is changed and the object is marked as needing to be redrawn. You can also force the redrawing of an element by calling setNeedsDisplay or setNeedsDisplayInRect on it. When the run loop restarts its cycle, all the elements that need redrawing are redrawn.

 For more information about buttons, refer to Apple's documentation, "Introduction to Buttons" at *http://developer.apple.com/mac/library/doc umentation/cocoa/Conceptual/Button/Button.html*.

You can also totally customize the drawing of your views by reimplementing the drawRect method on your NSView class. drawRect is called on a view when something about your view has changed or can be called manually.

Let's cover some other important Cocoa drawing concepts.

Graphics Context

In Cocoa, as in many GUIs, you don't apply visual traits directly to objects; that is, you don't say, "Draw this rectangle with a blue border" or "Write this text in italic." Instead, you define the traits in general for the whole window, using an abstraction called the *graphics context*. A typical sequence is:

1. Set the color in the graphics context to red.
2. Draw the background.
3. Set the color in the graphics context to black.
4. Draw a rectangle.
5. Etc..

The procedure may seem awkward, but it makes the best use of the hardware capabilities. A graphics context is thus a representation of the area onto which you're drawing. The context has a huge range of attributes, each of which takes on one value at a time, such as red or black. Its job is to set and hold all the information needed so a view can be drawn properly. It even saves its state before rendering so changes can be undone.

Most of the time, the graphics context you will interact with represents one of your application's windows, but the drawing destination can also refer to an image, an output device (i.e., a printer), a file, or an OpenGL surface. Cocoa maintains a separate graphics context per window and per thread. So, an application can have multiple contexts.

In a Cocoa application, graphics contexts for most types of canvas are represented by the NSGraphicsContext class. To access the current thread's graphics context, you can simply call NSGraphicsContext.currentContext. This is usually something you do when you implement your own drawRect method. The problem is that if you modify the current context, all other items drawn in the same thread will be affected by this change. For instance, if you are changing the fill color to red, all objects redrawn after the change will be redrawn with a red fill color. Here is an illustration of the problem:

```
framework 'Cocoa'
class CustomView < NSView

  def drawRect(rect)
    # draw a red background
    NSColor.redColor.set
    NSBezierPath.fillRect(rect)

    # draw a rectangle
    path = NSBezierPath.bezierPath
    path.lineWidth = 2
    # starting point
    path.moveToPoint [100, 50]
    # draw a rectangle
    path.lineToPoint [100, 100]
    path.lineToPoint [200, 100]
    path.lineToPoint [200, 50]
    # close the rectangle automatically
    path.closePath
    path.stroke
  end

end
```

```
application = NSApplication.sharedApplication

# create the window
frame  = [0.0, 0.0, 300, 200]
mask = NSTitledWindowMask | NSClosableWindowMask
window = NSWindow.alloc.initWithContentRect(frame,
        styleMask:mask,
        backing:NSBackingStoreBuffered,
        defer:false)

# assign a content view instance
content_view = CustomView.alloc.initWithFrame(frame)
window.contentView = content_view

# show the window
window.display
window.makeKeyAndOrderFront(nil)
window.orderFrontRegardless

application.run
```

The result is shown in Figure 5-12. The problem is that the rectangle we drew isn't visible.

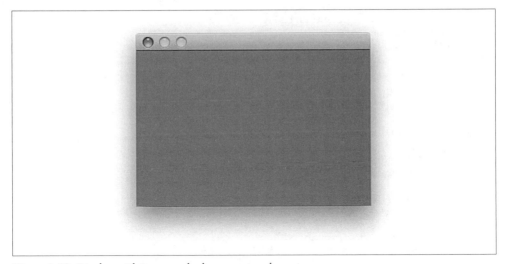

Figure 5-12. Display with improperly drawn rectangle

The source of the problem is quite easy to spot: we have switched the context color from black to red by using NSColor.redColor.set, but when we then draw the rectangle, the stroke is still red and we can't distinguish the rectangle.

An easy fix would obviously be to reset the color to black before drawing the stroke. While that would work for this simple example, imagine if you were changing more than two context attributes and you were drawing several items in the view. Having to manually reset the context every time would become quite challenging. A more robust approach is to save the current context, set a new context, draw what you want using the new context, and restore the old context. This is why Cocoa offers methods to save the context and then restore it:

```
framework 'Cocoa'
class CustomView < NSView

  def drawRect(rect)
    context = NSGraphicsContext.currentContext
    context.saveGraphicsState
    # draw a red background
    NSColor.redColor.set
    NSBezierPath.fillRect(rect)
    context.restoreGraphicsState

    # draw a rectangle
    path = NSBezierPath.bezierPath
    path.lineWidth = 2
    # starting point
    path.moveToPoint [100, 50]
    # draw a rectangle
    path.lineToPoint [100, 100]
    path.lineToPoint [200, 100]
    path.lineToPoint [200, 50]
    # close the rectangle automatically
    path.closePath
    path.stroke
  end

end

application = NSApplication.sharedApplication

# create the window
frame  = [0.0, 0.0, 300, 200]
mask = NSTitledWindowMask | NSClosableWindowMask
window = NSWindow.alloc.initWithContentRect(frame,
          styleMask:mask,
          backing:NSBackingStoreBuffered,
          defer:false)

# assign a content view instance
content_view = CustomView.alloc.initWithFrame(frame)
window.contentView = content_view

# show the window
window.display
window.makeKeyAndOrderFront(nil)
window.orderFrontRegardless

application.run
```

The result is shown in Figure 5-13. This time, the rectangle is visible.

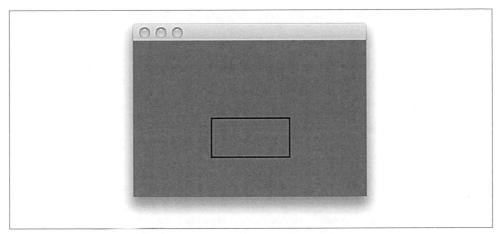

Figure 5-13. Display with all objects visible

And here is a more complete example, where we extract the graphics context switch into a method that can then be invoked for each object we draw:

```ruby
framework 'Cocoa'
class CustomView < NSView

  # Using a method yielding a block, we can keep
  # our code cleaner
  def temp_context(&block)
    context = NSGraphicsContext.currentContext
    context.saveGraphicsState
    yield
    context.restoreGraphicsState
  end

  def drawRect(rect)
    # draw a red background
    temp_context do
      NSColor.redColor.set
      NSBezierPath.fillRect(rect)
    end

    path = NSBezierPath.bezierPath
    path.lineWidth = 2
    # starting point
    path.moveToPoint [100, 50]
    # draw a rectangle
    path.lineToPoint [100, 100]
    path.lineToPoint [200, 100]
    path.lineToPoint [200, 50]
    # close the path automatically
    path.closePath

    # fill the content of the path in transparent white
    temp_context do
```

```
      NSColor.colorWithCalibratedWhite(0.9, alpha: 0.5).set
      NSBezierPath.fillRect([100, 50, 100, 50])
    end

    # draw the rectangle stroke after the content was filled
    path.stroke

    # draw some text, because we are changing the context shadow
    # we are doing that in a temp context
    temp_context do
      shadow = NSShadow.alloc.init
      shadow.shadowOffset = [4, -4]
      shadow.set
      font = NSFont.fontWithName("Helvetica", size:24)
      attributes = {NSFontAttributeName => font,
                      NSForegroundColorAttributeName => NSColor.whiteColor}
      "MacRuby Rocks".drawAtPoint([60, 120], withAttributes: attributes)
    end
  end

end

application = NSApplication.sharedApplication

# create the window
frame  = [0.0, 0.0, 300, 200]
mask = NSTitledWindowMask | NSClosableWindowMask | NSMiniaturizableWindowMask
window = NSWindow.alloc.initWithContentRect(frame,
          styleMask:mask,
          backing:NSBackingStoreBuffered,
          defer:false)

# assign a content view instance
content_view = CustomView.alloc.initWithFrame(frame)
window.contentView = content_view

# show the window
window.display
window.makeKeyAndOrderFront(nil)
window.orderFrontRegardless

application.run
```

The result is shown in Figure 5-14.

Figure 5-14. Result of the sample using an extracted context switch

The `temp_context` method takes, as its argument, a block of code that is executed after the current context is saved and before it is reset. The end result allows for a more expressive syntax and the code ends up being easier to maintain.

As a side note, as shown in the previous example, drawing text in a view is very simple. Probably the simplest way is to use `drawAtPoint`, as follows:

```
position = [60, 120]
"MacRuby Rocks".drawAtPoint(position, withAttributes: nil)
```

Other ways to draw text are to use `NSAttributedString` or `NSTextView`. I leave it up to you to explore further.

Images

To manipulate images, the Application Kit offers the `NSImage` class. With this class, you can load existing images from disk, draw image data into your views, create new images, scale and resize images, or convert images to any of several different formats.

A typical method that draws a simple image follows:

```
def drawRect(rect)
  NSColor.whiteColor.set
  NSBezierPath.fillRect(rect)
  img_url = NSURL.URLWithString('http://bit.ly/apple_logo_png')
  img = NSImage.alloc.initWithContentsOfURL(img_url)
  img.drawAtPoint([0,0],
  fromRect: NSZeroRect,
  operation: NSCompositeSourceOver,
  fraction: 1)
end
```

We start by setting the color to white and filling the background, then we specify the URL of the image to load. With the instance of NSURL ready, we just need to pass it to our NSImage constructor and we get an instance representing our image. Finally, we use an API similar to the one that drew text in the previous section.

In the call to drawAtPoint, the first parameter is the coordinate where we want to start drawing the picture (bottom left). Then we pass an empty rectangle represented by the NSZeroRect constant (passing [0,0,0,0] would have done the same thing). The operation parameter refers to the composing operation: in other words, the way the image should be composed. A list of operation constants is available in the NSImage class reference (*http://developer.apple.com/mac/library/documentation/cocoa/Refer ence/ApplicationKit/Classes/NSImage_Class/Reference/Reference.html#//apple_ref/c/ tdef/NSCompositingOperation*). Finally, the last parameter refers to the opacity. This ranges from 0 (totally transparent) to 1, totally opaque.

The code just shown appears near the top of the following example, which is a complete application using the image:

```
framework 'Cocoa'
class CustomView < NSView

  def drawRect(rect)
    NSColor.whiteColor.set
    NSBezierPath.fillRect(rect)
    img_url = NSURL.URLWithString('http://bit.ly/apple_logo_png')
    img = NSImage.alloc.initWithContentsOfURL(img_url)
    img.drawAtPoint([0,0], fromRect: NSZeroRect, operation: NSCompositeSourceOver,
    fraction: 1)
  end

end

application = NSApplication.sharedApplication

# create the window
frame  = [100, 100, 152, 186]
mask = NSTitledWindowMask | NSClosableWindowMask
window = NSWindow.alloc.initWithContentRect(frame,
          styleMask:mask,
          backing:NSBackingStoreBuffered,
          defer:false)

# assign a content view instance
content_view = CustomView.alloc.initWithFrame(frame)
window.contentView = content_view

# show the window
window.display
window.makeKeyAndOrderFront(nil)
window.orderFrontRegardless

application.run
```

Another way to display images is to use Interface Builder. Start by adding an image to your Xcode project. Then open your *.xib* file in Interface Builder and drag an instance of NSImageView (referred to as Image Well) from the Library to your UI. Select the new UI element and open the Inspector. In the Image View Attributes, use the scroll-down menu to pick your image. Voilà, you're done!

 NSImageView also optionally allows users to drag an image to your UI and display it.

## CHAPTER 6

Xcode

Apple likes to refer to Xcode as "the hub of your development experience." Technically, Xcode is a suite of developer tools designed to help developers write Cocoa applications. Most Cocoa developers spend their time in the Xcode IDE.

Xcode IDE

You don't need to use an IDE to write Cocoa apps. But you will more than likely want to use the tools in place to streamline development and avoid doing a lot of things manually. As of the writing of this chapter, Xcode doesn't support MacRuby as well as it supports Objective-C, but the key features are supported: MacRuby templates, schemes, and the integration with the Interface Builder suite.

To get acquainted with Xcode, you have the choice of starting a new project or opening an existing one. At this point, I will assume you have never used Xcode and you want to start a new MacRuby project.

Template

Start Xcode, click on Create a new Xcode project, select Application under Mac OS X, choose MacRuby Application (Figure 6-1), and click the Next button.

You will then be offered a few options, as shown in Figure 6-2:

Product Name
> The unique name of your application.

Company Identifier
> Your company ID using the reverse domain notation. This starts with the top-level domain, followed by a company or creator name, and then other subdomains, if any. For instance, a department called *iosdev.example.com* would put `com.exam ple.iosdev` here.

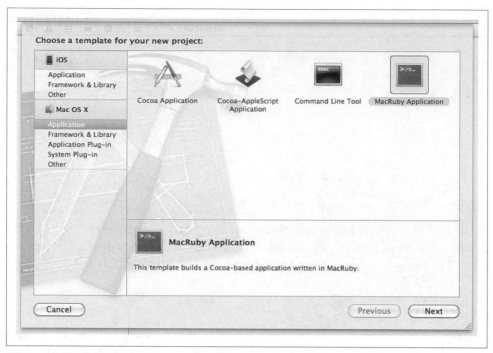

Figure 6-1. Xcode 4 template chooser

App Store Category

Optional category you want your application to appear under in the App Store.

Create Document-Based Application

A document-based application is an application (see *http://developer.apple.com/ library/mac/#documentation/cocoa/conceptual/Documents/Documents.html*)   re-volving around a document workflow. Think about a word processor or spread-sheet application. The user can create, edit, save, and print specific versions of a document. If your application requires this kind of workflow, you will want to enable this option. You will find a lot of information about document-based ap-plications online or in any decent Cocoa book. If enabled, you will be asked to provide a document class name and a document extension. The document class name will be used to create a class representing your document. The document extension is used for reference.

Use Core Data

Core Data is covered more in depth in Chapter 7. Enabling the core data option will set up your application with a delegate class that takes care of persistent stor-age. If you need to store data for your user, you might want to consider enabling this option.

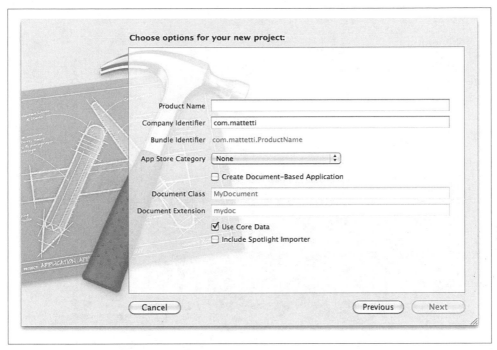

Figure 6-2. Xcode MacRuby application template option chooser

Include a Spotlight Importer

A Spotlight importer should be provided by all applications that support custom document formats. The Spotlight importer parses your document format for relevant information and assigns that information to the appropriate metadata keys, making your files' info available via Spotlight.

Choose a product name for your application and, after choosing the appropriate options, click Next. To keep things simple, I am going to assume you didn't enable Document-Based Application or Use Core Data. At this point, you will choose where to save your project and Xcode will automatically create a local *git repository* for it. Git is a distributed Source Control System that you can use to keep track of your changes, experiment in code branches, and share code with coworkers. You can also use a third-party service such as GitHub (*http://github.com*) to safely save and share your code online.

The Xcode interface is a bit overwhelming at first. You might not know where to start and what to do. Let's take a few minutes to visit the interface so you can understand the workflow.

The interface, called Workspace window, is broken down into four main areas (Figure 6-3):

- Navigator area
- Editor area
- Debug area
- Utility area

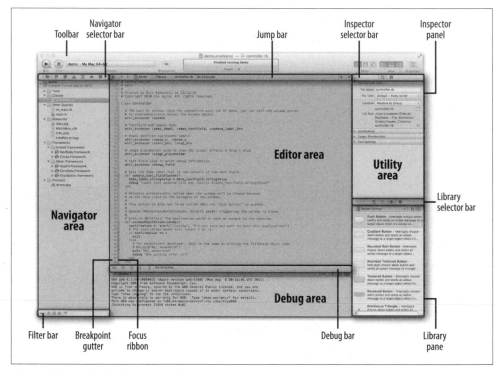

Figure 6-3. Xcode Workspace window

Navigator Area

The left part of the UI is called the Navigator area. It contains icons that allow you to switch from one navigator to the other. Seven navigators are available in Xcode 4:

Project navigator
  Shows you the files used in your application.

Symbol navigator
  Allows you to browse your Objective-C classes and methods (MacRuby isn't supported yet).

Search navigator
> Allows you to search your code or the frameworks you use.

Issue navigator
> Logs warning and errors during the build phases.

Debug navigator
> Allows you to navigate a debugging session in an Objective-C project (MacRuby isn't supported yet).

Breakpoint navigator
> Keeps track of your breakpoints (breakpoints in MacRuby aren't currently supported in Xcode).

Log navigator
> Allows you to navigate through previously generated logs.

If you look at the project navigator for a brand-new project, you will notice a few files, as shown in Figure 6-4. Here is a list of the files you will find in a new project:

app-name -Info.plist
> The application manifest file

MainMenu.xib
> The application UI file

rb_main.rb
> The application MacRuby main file (loaded by *main.m*)

AppDelegate.rb
> The delegate class that handles the default view's actions

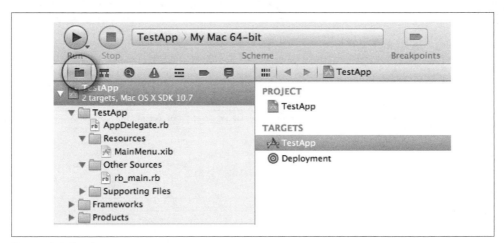

Figure 6-4. Xcode project navigator

The *rb_main.rb* file loads the Cocoa framework and all the Ruby files available in your build/scheme and starts the application.

The MacRuby main file globs the resource folder for MacRuby files (compiled or not) and loads them in the order they are found. If you have dependencies within your files, you might want to manually require some specific files in the *rb_main.rb* file or declare the dependencies at the top of each file (recommended). When the application is built, all the files are moved to the resources folder of the app. That is why the main file uses the `NSBundle.mainBundle.resourcePath.fileSystemRepre sentation` Cocoa API method to look for the MacRuby files there.

The Navigator pane is easy to figure out, so let's move on to an even more straightforward section: the editor.

Editor Area

The Editor (Figure 6-5) is the place where you edit your code. You can choose from three editor modes, denoted by icons (Figure 6-6):

Standard editor
    Normal code editing pane

Assistant editor
    Additional editing panes

Version editor
    Diff tool used to see the different versions/changes of a given file

```
#
#  rb_main.rb
#  testApp
#
#  Created by Matt Aimonetti on 3/13/11.
#  Copyright (c) 2011 m|a agile Consulting. All rights reserved.
#

# Loading the Cocoa framework. If you need to load more frameworks, you can
# do that here too.
framework 'Cocoa'

# Loading all the Ruby project files.
main = File.basename(__FILE__, File.extname(__FILE__))
dir_path = NSBundle.mainBundle.resourcePath.fileSystemRepresentation
Dir.glob(File.join(dir_path, '*.{rb,rbo}')).map { |x| File.basename(x, File.extname(x)) }.uniq.each do |path|
  if path != main
    require(path)
  end
end

# Starting the Cocoa main loop.
NSApplicationMain(0, nil)
```

Figure 6-5. Xcode Editor

Figure 6-6. Xcode Editor modes

Because Xcode's Ruby support isn't great, I personally use MacVim (*http://code.google.com/p/macvim/*) to edit Ruby code, and I set up the "Open with External Editor" feature to use MacVim from within Xcode.

By default, the line numbers aren't displayed. If you want to display them, open the Xcode preferences, choose the Text Editing tab, and select "Show Line numbers."

If you wish to create custom snippets, you will need to go into the Code Snippet Library and create your own. (The Code Snippet Library is available from the Utility area.)

Debug Area

Located at the bottom of the screen, the Debug area displays debug information and the data printed out by the application (Figure 6-7).

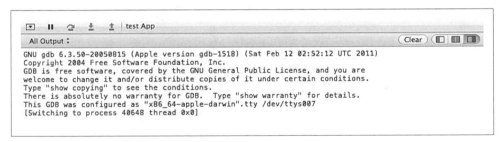

Figure 6-7. Xcode Debug area

You can print data to the Debug area by using Ruby's `puts` or Cocoa's `NSLog`:

```
puts "It is #{Time.now}"
NSLog "It is week number: %s" % Time.now.strftime("%W")
```

The output is as follows:

```
It is 2011-03-20 21:04:03 -0700
2011-03-20 21:04:03.774 test App[40827:903] It is week number: 11
```

As you can see, the `NSLog` call is timestamped, and the app name is printed along with a reference ID before the string you request? This area of the workspace is really straightforward and shouldn't cause you any trouble.

Utility Area

The Utility area, located on the right side of the screen, can seem complex at times. The reason is that this area is contextual: in other words, the options will change depending on what you are editing. As you can see in Figure 6-8, the Inspector selector bar has only two top tabs, the one we are on (File Inspector) and the Quick Help tab.

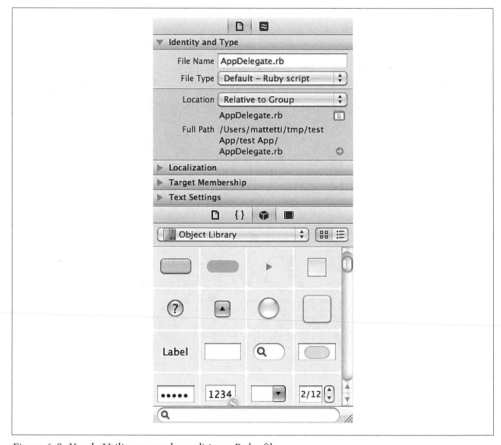

Figure 6-8. Xcode Utility area when editing a Ruby file

The bottom part of the Utility area, called the Library pane, on the other hand, has four tabs. The icons in this pane, shown in Figure 6-8, from left to right, refer to:

- File Template Library (list of file templates)
- Code Snippet Library (list of code snippets)
- Object Library (list of UI-related objects)
- Media Library (list of media to use in your app)

Now, if we were to edit a UI file such as an *.xib* file, the top menu (Inspector pane) would look quite different (Figure 6-9).

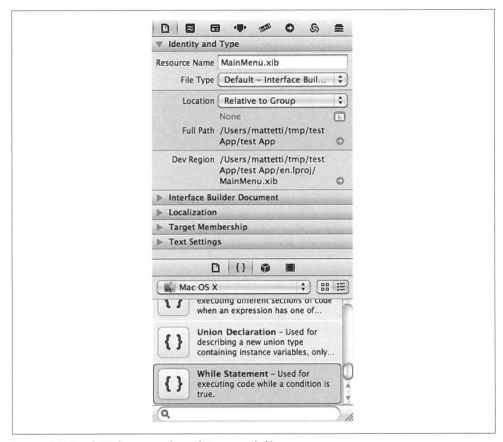

Figure 6-9. Xcode Utility area when editing an .xib file

This time, in addition to File inspect and Quick Help, we have six more tabs at the very top:

- Identity Inspector (overall settings of a given UI element)
- Attributes Inspector (attribute details of a given UI element)
- Size Inspector (lets you define the size and resizing behaviors of a given UI element)
- Connections Inspector (relationships with other objects)
- Bindings Inspector (binding details, discussed in "Bindings" on page 80)
- View Effects Inspector (appearance settings for a given item)

As you can see, the Utility area is useful mainly when editing a UI. As a matter of fact, I hide this area most of the time and display it only when editing my UI. There are two ways to show and hide areas via the View menu and via the workspace buttons (Figure 6-10).

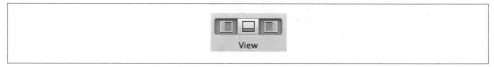

Figure 6-10. Xcode view selector

## CHAPTER 7

Core Data

Core Data is Cocoa's model and framework for manipulating and storing data. In a nutshell, Core Data provides a nice way to handle relational object persistence without having to worry about the underlying storage.

What do you get from it?

- Key-value coding and key-value observing
- Validation
- Undo/redo support
- Relationship maintenance
- Querying, filtering, and grouping
- Version tracking and optimistic locking
- Schema migration
- A memory-optimized solution
- Integration with Apple's tool chain (XCode, Interface Builder, and Instruments)

But remember that Core Data is not a database replacement. Even though you can set Core Data to use SQLite as a data store, Core Data doesn't support sophisticated database operations such as joins. All it supports is the basic CRUD operations. See the Wikipedia entry for CRUD interface (*http://en.wikipedia.org/wiki/Create,_read,_update _and_delete*). If you are interested in using a database such as SQLite, look at the various Ruby ORMs such as Sequel (*http://sequel.rubyforge.org/*).

Data Model

At the heart of Core Data is a rich data modeling solution based on simple tools and configuration. The modeling is pretty close to a database design and if you have any experience with databases, you should be able to adapt really quickly.

The best way to understand how Core Data works is to create a simple data model. Let's build a simple example application: a movie library. At the end of this chapter, we will have built a persisting (saved to disk) movie library that looks like the one shown in Figure 7-1.

Figure 7-1. Movie library using Core Data

To get there, we are going to use Xcode. It will dramatically reduce the amount of code we have to write. As a matter of fact, we are probably going to write less than 50 lines of code in total! Start Xcode and create a new MacRuby application called CoreDataExample, and don't forget to enable the Use Core Data option. This template handles persistence through a file with the extension *.xcdatamodel* and an application delegate class.

The Data Model and the Entity

An entity in Core Data is a bit like a container that structures the objects it holds. It can be loosely compared to a database table, but it differs in some major ways. For instance, entities may be arranged in an inheritance hierarchy and are directly tied to a class.

Let's create an entity for our movies. Browse the model folder; you should see a file called *CoreDataExample.xcdatamodeld*. Select this file. You should see something similar to Figure 7-2. As we build our entity, this file will hold the data structure that Core Data will use.

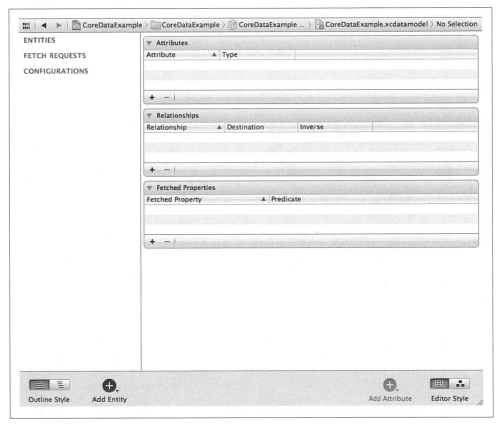

Figure 7-2. View of a blank xcdatamodel file in Xcode 4

Click Add Entity and name the new entity `Movie`.

We don't need to change the defaults. The entity is represented by the `NSManagedObject` class and doesn't inherit from any other entities (see the details in the Data Model Inspector).

 The Data Model Inspector is available in the Utilities area. If you can't see it, you can display it via the top menu: View → Utilities → Data Model Inspector.

Adding Attributes

An attribute is something describing data, such as a movie's title. Attributes are to an entity as columns are to a table: until we add attributes, an entity is useless. Attributes can be added different ways and are edited using the Data Model Inspector. After selecting the entity, click the big Add Attribute button at the bottom of the screen. Add the following attributes with the appropriate settings:

- title (string, required)
- genre (string, optional)
- imagePath (string, optional)
- release_date (date, optional, minimum value: 01/011/1895)

At this point, your model should look like Figure 7-3 in Xcode 4.

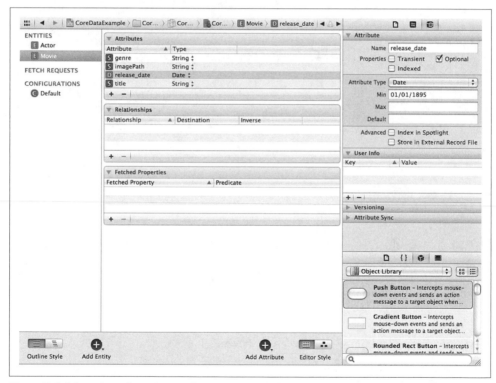

Figure 7-3. Movies' attributes in Xcode 4

Relationships

Relationships between entities are another very important aspect of model design, just as foreign keys provide relationships between database tables. An example of a relationship in our case is between a movie and actors. A movie can have many actors. So we'll model this as a one-to-many relationship between a movie and an actor. (In real life, you'd have to do something more complicated, because an actor can also be in many movies, but we'll stick to one-to-many for now.)

First, we'll create a second entity, an `Actor` with the following attributes:

- `name` (string)
- `gender` (string, default value: Female)
- `fictional` (Boolean, default value: NO)

We will now create a relationship between `Movie` and `Actor`, as illustrated in Figure 7-4.

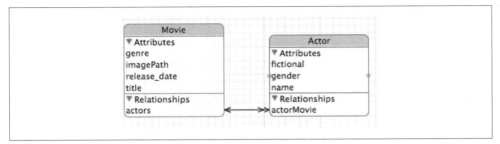

Figure 7-4. Relationships between our entities

Select `Movie` and add a new relationship called `actors`. Set the destination to `Actor`—don't worry about the inverse relationship for now—and set the relationship to be optional and plural (To-Many Relationship).

Now select `Actor` and create a new relationship. The new relationship should be named `actorMovie` with `Movie` as a destination and `actors` as the inverse relationship. Make sure the Optional checkbox is enabled and the Plural checkbox is not enabled. You can then see the final relationship in Xcode as Figure 7-5. Notice that the `Movie`'s inverse relationship has been set automatically.

Setting Up Controllers

We'll spend most of the rest of this chapter in what used to be called Interface Builder, the UI editor for Xcode. Since Xcode 4, Interface Builder is built into Xcode. Depending on the version you are using, click or double-click the *.xib* file shown in the Xcode navigator. What we want to do is create a UI that will let us create and edit existing movies and their related data.

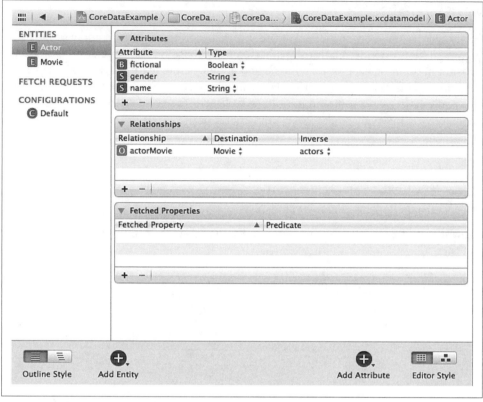

Figure 7-5. The Movie/Actor relationship viewed from the Movie entity

The first step is to create a UI object that will retrieve and store all our movies. The best object to use for that is `NSArrayController`. This class, which is compatible with Cocoa bindings (it conforms to a protocol allowing you to automatically bind UI elements to objects), manages a collection of objects and provides selection management and sorting capabilities. We will need two array controllers—one for our movies and one for their actors:

1. Drag and drop an `NSArrayController` instance to the Object list, in the editor.

2. Edit the controller's attributes to look like Figure 7-6, by doing the following:
   - Change the mode from Class to Entity.
   - Name the entity `Movie`.
   - Make sure the Prepare Content flag is on.

3. Change the Array Controller's label to "movies" (use the identity label field in Identity Inspector)

4. Finally, edit the `movies` array controller binding's parameters to bind the Managed Object Context to the `AppDelegate` class. The Model Key Path should be automatically set to `managedObjectContext`, as shown in Figure 7-7.

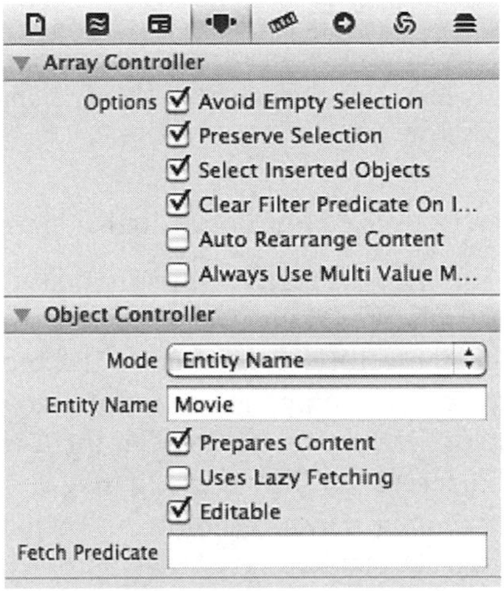

Figure 7-6. Array controller attributes property set

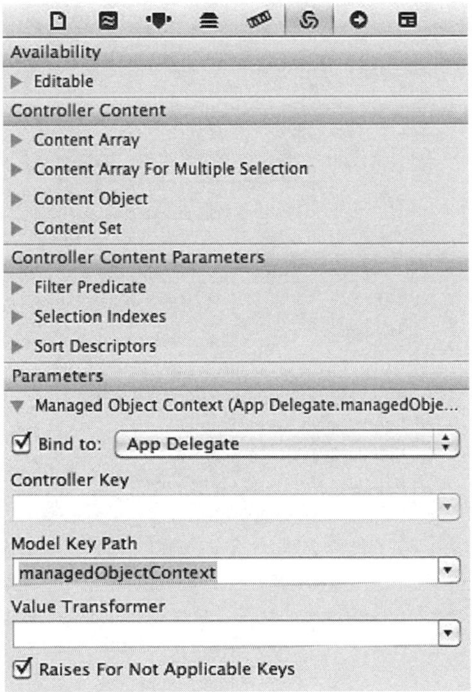

Figure 7-7. Array controller bindings property set

The Object Library, where you will find NSArrayController, is inside the Utility area. You can display it via the top menu: View → Utilities → Object Library. If you want a better view of the objects and placeholders, click the small arrow at the bottom of the long column of icons to the left of the UI preview.

We've finished with the Movie entity. Now go through a similar process for Actor.

Create an NSArrayController called actors with its mode set to the Actor entity name and the Prepare Content flag checked. However, this time the bindings will be slightly different. We want to bind the actor's controller to the movie's actors so we don't display all the actors in memory, but only the ones related to the current edited movie. To do that, bind the Content Set value to movies. Set the Controller Key to selection and the Model Key Path to actors, as shown in Figure 7-8. Don't forget to also bind the Managed Object Context in the parameters subsection to the AppDelegate class and the Model Key Path to managedObjectContext.

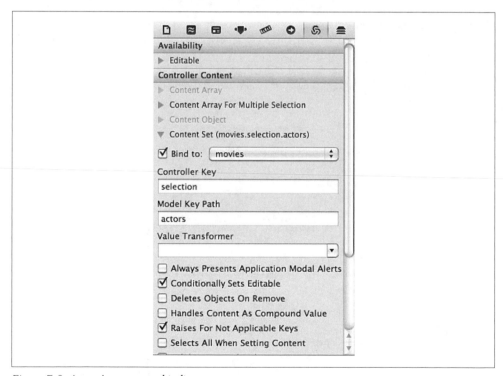

Figure 7-8. Actors' content set bindings

User Interface

So far, we've designed our model and created two array containers to hold our data. It's now time to add some UI elements. The end result should look like Figure 7-9.

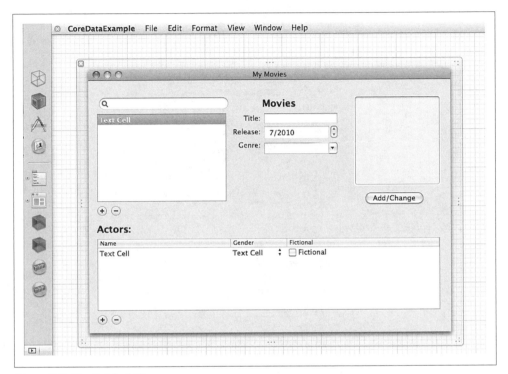

Figure 7-9. The finished UI

Movies

We'll start with the Table View, which will list all the movies. The goal here is to allow sorting and selection of movies:

1. Drag and drop a Table View into your main window.

2. Expand the Scroll View - Table View tab to access its Table View.

3. Change the attributes (no headers, 1 column, source list highlight) to match Figure 7-10.

4. Expand the Table View to access its Table Column

5. Bind the table view's value to movies.arrangedObjects.title, as shown in Figure 7-11.

6. Change the attributes to have a sort key and a selector, as shown in Figure 7-12.

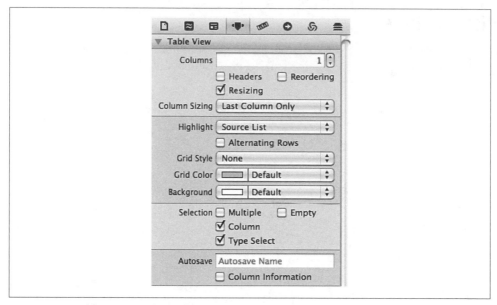

Figure 7-10. Table View attributes for Movies

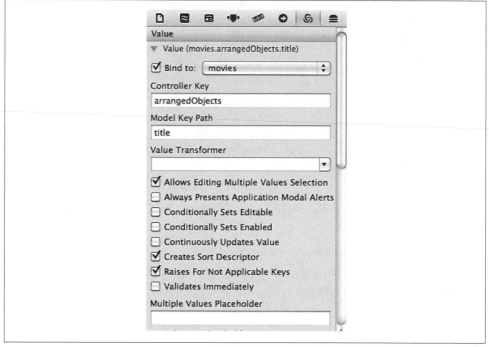

Figure 7-11. Table Column's bindings

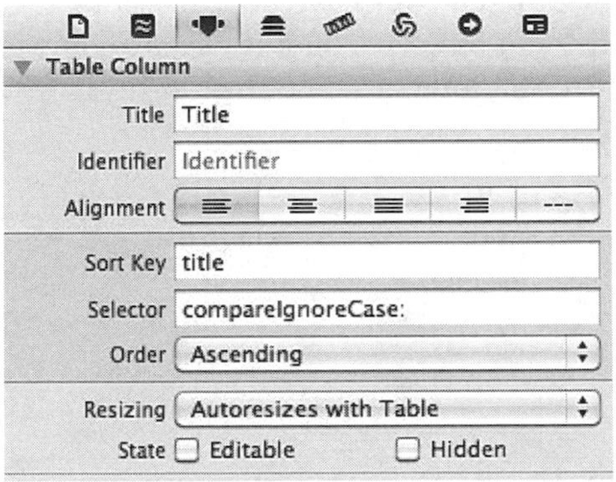

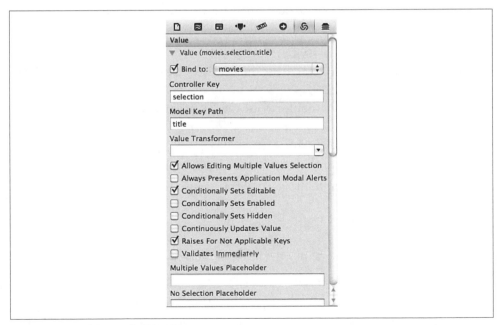

Figure 7-12. Table Column's attributes

Now that we have a way to display our movie titles, we need a way to display more information and to edit this information. We are going to add three fields: one for the title, one for the release date, and one for the genre. Assign a label to identify each field and use a `Text Field` data type for the title, a `Date Picker` for the release date, and a `Combo Box` for the genre.

Each field's value needs to be bound to the related array controller selection's attribute. For instance, the title's text field is shown in Figure 7-13.

Figure 7-13. Title's text field binding

The Combo Box is slightly different, since we need to define the available values. This can be done in the Model, but to keep it simple, we are going to hardcode the values, as shown in Figure 7-14 (don't forget to bind the box to `movies.selection.genre`).

Figure 7-14. Hardcoded Combo Box items

We also need two buttons, one to add a new movie and one to remove an existing movie. The buttons' actions must be bound to the movies array controller:

1. Add two buttons to the UI (the style doesn't matter).
2. Edit the first button's attributes to use the `NSAddTemplate` image and a "Round Rect" bezel.
3. Edit the second button's attributes to use the `NSRemoveTemplate` image and a Round Rect bezel.
4. Select both buttons. Click Editor → Size to Fit.
5. Set the + button's selector to the `movies` array controller `add:` action.
6. Set the - button's selector to the `movies` array controller `remove:` action.

 To set the buttons' selector, right-click a button, expand the Sent Actions section, click the round icon on the same line as the selector, drag the cursor to the array of your choice, and then choose the appropriate action.

Build and run the application to make sure it works fine. You should be able to add a new movie by clicking the + button, then select the new row and edit the attributes. Try it a few times to make sure everything works as expected.

Art Cover

What would a movie library be without art covers? We are going to write some code to handle the movie covers. We need to let our users choose a cover and we need to display it when the movie is selected. That will actually be the only code manually written in this chapter.

To give the user the option to add/change/display movie covers, we need to start writing our action and wire it to our views. The wiring is done through an outlet (IBOutlet) defined in our AppDelegate class and keeping a reference to our movies NSArrayController. MacRuby makes that really easy: just define an attribute writer or attribute accessor, and Xcode will see it as an outlet. By default, the MacRuby Core Data Application template defines an attribute accessor for the main window. This creates a getter and a setter for the window, allowing us to call it from within our code as window. We now need to add an accessor/outlet for movies, the array controller we have created in the view:

```
class AppDelegate
  attr_accessor :window
  attr_accessor :movies
```

Don't forget to wire the AppDelegate movies outlet to the movies controller (right-click AppDelegate in the UI editor and connect the two objects). We can now write the action code as follows:

```
def add_image(sender)
  movie = movies.selectedObjects.lastObject
  return unless movie
  panel = NSOpenPanel.openPanel
  panel.canChooseDirectories = false
  panel.canCreateDirectories = false
  panel.allowsMultipleSelection = false

  panel.beginSheetModalForWindow window, completionHandler: Proc.new{|result|
    return if (result == NSCancelButton)
    path = panel.filename
    # use a GUID to avoid conflicts
    guid = NSProcessInfo.processInfo.globallyUniqueString
    # set the destination path in the support folder
    dest_path = applicationFilesDirectory.URLByAppendingPathComponent(guid)
    dest_path = dest_path.relativePath
    error = Pointer.new(:id)
    NSFileManager.defaultManager.copyItemAtPath(path, toPath:dest_path, error:error)
    NSApplication.sharedApplication.presentError(error[0]) if error[0]
    movie.setValue(dest_path, forKey:"imagePath")
  }

end
```

Let's break it down to make sure everything is clear:

```
movie = movies.selectedObjects.lastObject
return unless movie
```

We start by fetching the selected movie from the `movies` `NSArrayController`. If nothing is selected, we just exit the action.

Then we open a panel (see *http://developer.apple.com/library/mac/#documentation/Cocoa/Reference/ApplicationKit/Classes/NSOpenPanel_Class/Reference/Reference.html*) and set its settings:

```
panel = NSOpenPanel.openPanel
panel.canChooseDirectories = false
panel.canCreateDirectories = false
panel.allowsMultipleSelection = false
```

Finally, we call the `beginSheetModalForWindow` API, which takes a C block as its last argument. If you need to refresh your memory concerning C blocks, refer to "Blocks" on page 137.

Here is the API call:

```
panel.beginSheetModalForWindow window, completionHandler: Proc.new{|result|
  return if (result == NSCancelButton)
  path = panel.filename
  # use a GUID to avoid conflicts
  guid = NSProcessInfo.processInfo.globallyUniqueString
  # set the destination path in the support folder
  dest_path = applicationFilesDirectory.URLByAppendingPathComponent(guid)
  dest_path = dest_path.relativePath
  error = Pointer.new(:id)
  NSFileManager.defaultManager.copyItemAtPath(path, toPath:dest_path, error:error)
  NSApplication.sharedApplication.presentError(error[0]) if error[0]
  movie.setValue(dest_path, forKey:"imagePath")
}
```

We are calling `beginSheetModalForWindow` on `panel` and passing two arguments: the Outlet pointing to our window and a proc that is called when the modal is closed. The proc takes an argument that reflects the button pressed by the user. The Objective-C method signature of this API looks like this:

```
- (void)beginSheetModalForWindow:(NSWindow *)window
              completionHandler:(void (^)(NSInteger result))handler
```

If the handler is passed a result matching the constant value `NSCancelButton`, the user has changed his mind and we should exit the action. Otherwise, we collect the selected filename from the panel. We also create a destination path by appending a global unique ID to the `applicationFilesDirectory` path. `applicationFilesDirectory`, defined in the application template, specifies where all the application's files are saved. In this case, the value of `applicationFilesDirectory` is *~/Library/Application Support/CoreDataExample/*.

Once we know where we want to save the file, we can copy it using `NSFileManager`. We then check that the error pointer doesn't contain any errors. If it does, we present them to the user via the `NSApp.presentError` call. Finally, we set the `imagePath` of our movie.

Now it's time to wire our brand new action in the UI.

Start by dragging an Image Well (instance of `NSImageView`) from the Object Library to the main window. This will display the art cover once the user chooses it. Bind its Value Path to `movies.selection.imagePath`. In other words, bind the Image Well's Value Path to `movies`, and set the Controller Key to "selection" and the Model Key Path to image-Path, as shown in Figure 7-15.

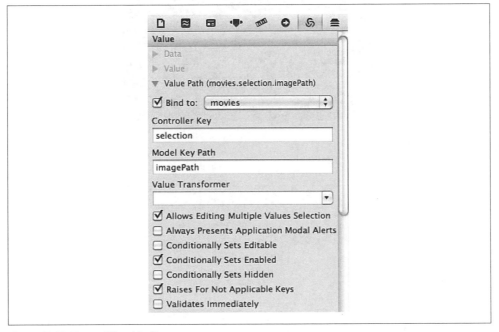

Figure 7-15. Image View bindings

Now that the bindings are set, the UI will display the image from our data store. But we still need to define a way for the user to use the code we just wrote and let him add or change a movie's cover. If you've followed along carefully, you should be able to implement the next step on your own. But just in case, here it is:

1. Add a new button
2. Wire the button action to our `add_image:` method as shown Figure 7-16.

Your UI should look similar to what's shown in Figure 7-17. We've built the table view, the various buttons, and the image preview, but we are missing the search box (we'll work on that last) and the bottom part.

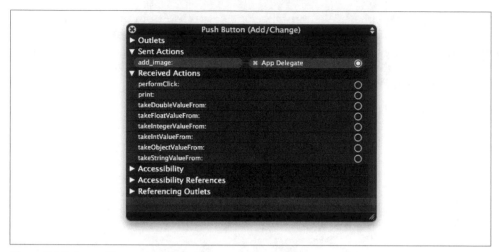

Figure 7-16. Image Button Action binding

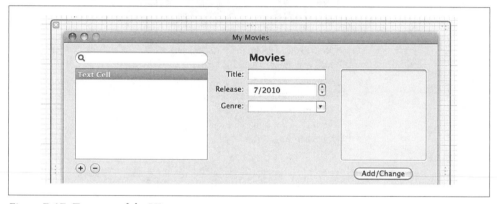

Figure 7-17. Top part of the UI

Let's focus next on the bottom part of the UI (Figure 7-18).

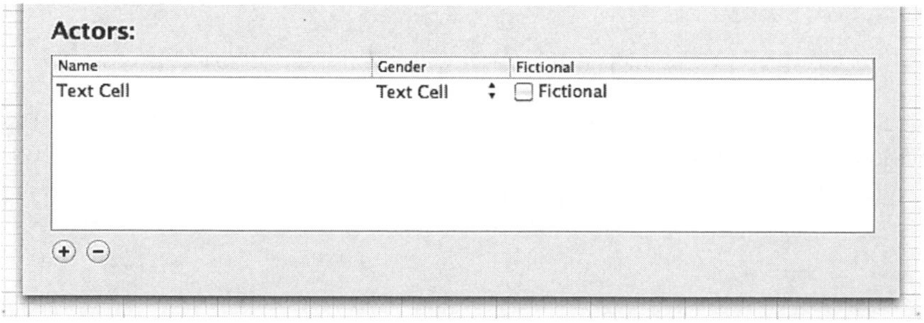

Figure 7-18. Bottom part of the UI

Actors

The lower part of the UI shows the actors for a selected movie. We are going to set a new Table View exactly the same way as the movies' table view, but instead of binding its elements to the movies array controller, we are going to bind them to the actors array controller.

Because we just went through these steps, we won't go into the binding details. You can look at the example source code if you can't set the bindings properly.

Figure 7-19 shows a screenshot of the actor's name column.

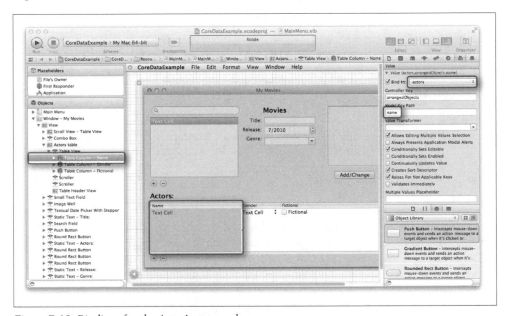

Figure 7-19. Bindings for the Actor's name column

Something you might not know how to do yet is to use a different type of column cell. As you can see in the example, the actors' table uses three different cell types: Text Field Cell, Combo Box Cell, and Button Cell.

For that, you first need to add a new column, select the actors' table view, and open the inspector. Once there, set the total amount of columns you want (Figure 7-20).

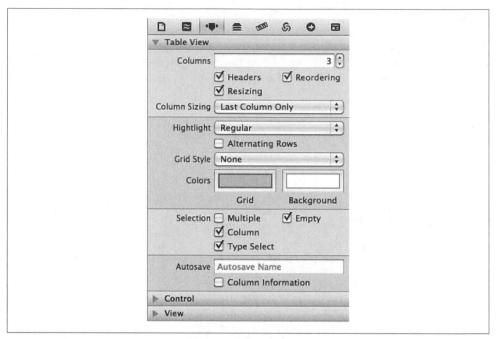

Figure 7-20. Table View columns settings

Then extend the newly added column, choose the cell, and open the identity tab. In the Custom Class field pick another cell class such as NSButtonCell, NSComboBoxCell, NSSliderCell, or NSImageCell (Figure 7-21).

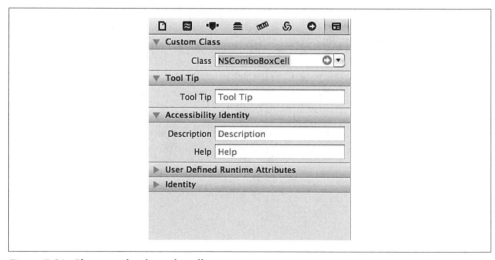

Figure 7-21. Changing the class of a cell

You also need to bind the combo box's value to `actors.selection.gender` and the button cell's value to `actors.selection.fictional`.

Search

The last missing part is the search field at the top right of our UI. The search field allows us to search for movies by name. Drag and drop the Search Field icon (representing the `NSSearchField` class) from the Object Library to the UI. Once the field is positioned, we need to set some bindings so the text entered in the text field is used to search the movies by title.

As shown in Figure 7-22, we need to bind the search predicate value to the `Movies` array controller. Apple has a lot of documentation about using predicates (see *http://developer .apple.com/library/mac/#documentation/Cocoa/Conceptual/Predicates/predicates.html*) In this example, we'll just scratch the surface.

Figure 7-22. Search field bindings

As you can see in Figure 7-22, when binding the search to the `Movies` array, we also set the Controller Key value to `filterPredicate` (this is called a *predicate binding*). This means we are going to set a predicate for an array controller to filter the content array (in our case `Movies`). This process is also well documented by Apple (see *http://developer .apple.com/library/mac/#documentation/Cocoa/Reference/CocoaBindingsRef/Cocoa BindingsRef.html*). The last missing piece is the predicate format, which is a bit like the query string. In our case, because we want to find any movies containing the string entered in the search field, the predicate format looks like `title contains $value`, where `$value` is replaced by the value of the text field.

 You can set multiple predicates, and the user can use the arrow in the search field to choose the desired predicate. If you want to do that, you need to make sure to set a Display Name value so the user knows how he is filtering the data.

Persistence

Data persistence is handled for you by the template provided by MacRuby. Let's look at the different parts involved in providing data persistence.

Managed Object Model

Before even talking about persisting the user data, we need to talk about the Managed Object Model, also known as "mom." When we worked on the Core Data app, we designed our model by editing an *.xcdatamodeld* file: *CoreDataExample.xcdatamodeld*. In the background, Xcode actually uses a source directory where all the info is stored. When we compile our app, each file in the source directory is compiled into a *mom* file and stored into a folder with the *.momd* extension (as in "mom deployment" directory). This is how the application knows about the data structures and relationships to use.

If you look at your compiled application (the *.app* file), right-click it, choose Show Package Contents, and drill down to Contents/Resources, you will see the *momd* folder and its *mom* file (Figure 7-23).

Name	Date Modified	Size	Kind
AppDelegate.rb	Today, 9:51 AM	8 KB	Ruby source
▼ CoreDataExample.momd	Today, 9:51 AM	--	Folder
CoreDataExample.mom	Today, 9:51 AM	8 KB	Comp... Model
VersionInfo.plist	Today, 9:51 AM	4 KB	Property List
▶ en.lproj	Today, 9:51 AM	--	Folder
rb_main.rb	Today, 9:51 AM	4 KB	Ruby source

Figure 7-23. Contents of the Resources directory

The template has a method that finds the *momd* deployment directory and exposes it to the rest of the code.

The mom compiler is also available outside of Xcode, via the command line: */Developer/usr/bin/momc*

Managed Object Context

The Managed Object Context is at the heart of the Core Data stack. The main job of the context is to manage a collection of objects. It is used under the covers to create and fetch managed objects, and to manage undo and redo operations.

All the data is stored in memory and is then flushed to the persistent store when the context is saved. The Managed Object Context is basically what you interact with when editing Core Data values. It is a very powerful layer that works great and that you don't have to worry about when writing Core Data application using the MacRuby template. That's because the template takes care of setting the context and making it available for you.

To summarize, the Managed Object Context handles the interactions with Core Data managed objects in a very transparent way and delegates the persistence to a persistent store via its coordinator.

Persistent Store Coordinator

The persistent store coordinator is an API on top of different types of persistent stores such as XML, SQLite, binary, or in-memory. The coordinator acts as a broker between one or many Managed Object Contexts and one or many persistent stores. In other words, they associate Managed Object Models to persistent stores via the use of the models' contexts.

You can run multiple coordinators connecting to one or many stores, depending on what you want to do. By default, the MacRuby Core Data template sets only one coordinator, which uses an XML store. If you look at the *AppDelegate.rb* file that is generated with your Core Data app, you will notice the `persistentStoreCoordinator` method. Here is how the store is set:

```
url = directory.URLByAppendingPathComponent("CoreDataExample.storedata")
@persistentStoreCoordinator = NSPersistentStoreCoordinator.alloc. \
        initWithManagedObjectModel(mom)
@persistentStoreCoordinator.addPersistentStoreWithType(NSXMLStoreType,
                                        configuration:nil,
                                        URL:url,
                                        options:nil,
                                        error:error)
```

You can easily change that default if you decide to use another store.

Workflow

Now that we have examined all the different moving pieces, let's see how they come together. In our interface, we bound our movies' and actors' array controllers to the `AppDelegate`'s Managed Object Context (see Figure 7-7) and we mapped these controllers to entities in our Managed Object Model. By wiring these few things, we gained access to our model and its context. The Xcode template defines a few other hooks such as the delegation of the window undo manager to the Model Object Context, giving us "free" undo and redo via the context. The template also defines the `saveAction` that commits the context changes to the persistent store and a hook into the app termination process that triggers the saving of the managed context to the persistent store (see the `applicationShouldTerminate` method in the *AppDelegate.rb* file).

The good news is that the wiring needed at the developer level is very simple and, unless you have custom needs, the defaults work fine. If you want to know the difference between the various persistent stores and why and how to run many persistent store coordinators, or if you want to dig further into Core Data, I strongly encourage you to look at the documentation provided by Apple on the topic.

## CHAPTER 8

One Step Deeper

In Chapter 7, we looked at the basics of MacRuby. You are now ready to get started with developing complex apps. Depending on the way you approach learning, you might want to first jump to hacking or you might want to first learn more advanced techniques. This chapter will focus on some advanced aspects of MacRuby that will help you go deeper in your MacRuby knowledge. Feel free to skip this chapter and come back to it later on if that makes more sense to you.

Selectors

In Objective-C, methods are identified by *selectors*. A selector is composed of the name of the method and keywords specifying the arguments to the method. If you have two methods that are the same except for the number and/or kind of arguments they accept, Objective-C treats them as separate methods. In Ruby, a method is specified by its name alone. The sort of arguments passed to a method have no bearing on which Ruby method is called. Therefore, to support the Objective-C method calling style, MacRuby extends Ruby to create Objective-C selectors from the arguments passed to a function. The examples in this chapter are meant to explain MacRuby's method overloading, (see the Wikipedia entry for method overloading at *http://en.wikipedia.org/wiki/Method _overloading*), which is not something Ruby programmers normally deal with. Look carefully at the examples. The method names are always the same, and only the expected parameters are different.

Let's imagine that we have a `Player` class and that it defines a method called `add_contact` that takes two parameters: a name and a hash with a `tags` key. This method adds a new contact to the player contact list, tagging the new contact with the passed tags. We can also define another method called `add_contact` that takes two different parameters: a name and a hash with the `location` key:

```
class Player
  def add_contact(name, tags:contact_tags)
    @name = name
    @tags = contact_tags
```

```
      "new contact #{name} was added and tagged."
    end

    def add_contact(name, location:contact_location)
      @name = name
      @contact_location = contact_location
      "new contact #{name} was added and located."
    end
  end
```

There are four different ways to call the add_contact method:

```
player = Player.new
player.add_contact('Matt', tags: ['Ruby', 'Cocoa'])
# => new contact Matt was added and tagged.
player.add_contact('Matt', location: 'San Diego')
# => new contact Matt was added and located.
player.add_contact('Matt')
# => NoMethodError: undefined method 'add_contact'
player.add_contact('Matt', tags: ['Ruby'], location: 'San Diego') # => NoMethodError:
```

As you can see, the method signature/selector used will determine which method to dispatch. If we want to define a method for the last two examples, we can use the following:

```
class Player
  def add_contact(name, options={})
    # do something with the options passed
  end
end
```

This is important to understand, because you will often need to use selectors in MacRuby when your code relies on Cocoa frameworks.

To help you interpret existing Cocoa documentation for use with Ruby methods, here is an extract of the NSMutableString documentation:

---

insertString:atIndex:

Inserts into the receiver the characters of a given string at a given location.

```
    - (void)insertString:(NSString *)aString atIndex:(NSUInteger)anIndex
```

Parameters

aString

The string to insert into the receiver. aString must not be nil.

anIndex

The location at which aString is inserted. The location must not exceed the bounds of the receiver.

This is how you call this method using an Objective-C selector (in this case, *atIndex*):

```
"Ruby".insertString("Mac", atIndex:0)  # => "MacRuby"
```

 You can get the same results by calling an entirely different method. The Ruby `insert` method produces the same result if used as follows: `"Ruby".insert(0, "Mac")`

Hopefully this example helps you understand how to use the Cocoa documentation to port and implement Objective-C selectors, especially in the case of delegates.

If you remember the "Hello, World!" example we wrote at the beginning of this chapter, you might remember that we passed a selector to the button action. The selector was a string with the method name, followed by a colon (the colon was needed because the method had arguments). You might wonder why we called it a selector, whereas in this section, selectors seem different.

The source of confusion is that in Objective-C, *selector* has two meanings. It can refer to a method signature or the unique identifier associated with a method. By the first definition, methods that take different arguments have different selectors, whereas, by the second, all methods with the same name have the same selector.

Blocks

Another important part of the Ruby syntax is the concept of *blocks*. MacRuby has blocks as well as procs and lambdas. They are all commonly referred as *closures*. Let's look at some example code to understand this powerful concept:

```
days = ['Sunday', 'Monday', 'Tuesday', 'Wednesday', 'Thursday', 'Friday', 'Saturday']
days.each_with_index do |day, index|
  puts "day #{index + 1} of the week is #{day}"
end
```

Running the code above will result in the following output:

```
day 1 of the week is Sunday
day 2 of the week is Monday
day 3 of the week is Tuesday
day 4 of the week is Wednesday
day 5 of the week is Thursday
day 6 of the week is Friday
day 7 of the week is Saturday
```

`days` is an array on which we are calling the `each_with_index` method and passing it a *block*. A block is like the body of an anonymous method that is being passed to a defined method as a parameter. The block is invoked as the defined method executes.

In this case, the block is delimited by the `do`/`end` keywords, but you can also define blocks using curly brackets, as shown here:

```
days = ['Sunday', 'Monday', 'Tuesday', 'Wednesday', 'Thursday', 'Friday', 'Saturday']
days.each_with_index{ |day, index|  puts "day #{index + 1} => #{day}" }
```

This code will generate the following output:

```
day 1 => Sunday
day 2 => Monday
day 3 => Tuesday
day 4 => Wednesday
day 5 => Thursday
day 6 => Friday
day 7 => Saturday
```

each and each_with_index are iterators—methods that invoke a block of code for each of its contained items. In the case of each_with_index, two arguments are passed to the block on each iteration: an array item's value and its index. The block called in the previous example prints out a string, interpolating the two passed values.

 There are a few different ways to use closures in MacRuby, but the examples shown in this section are the most common usage you will encounter.

When using blocks, you need to be careful about the scope you are operating on. When called, a block has access to the context it's being called on and will operate on it. Here is a simple example:

```
macruby_genius = 'Laurent'
developers = ['laurent', 'josh', 'matt', 'jordan']
developers = developers.map do |dev|
  macruby_genius = dev
end
macruby_genius # => "jordan"
```

As you can see, each iteration of the array redefines the macruby_genius variable defined earlier. So the value assigned last remains as part of the surrounding context after the do loop ends. A block is different from a method, which implicitly creates its own local context, as shown in the following example:

```
macruby_genius = 'Laurent'
developers = ['laurent', 'josh', 'matt', 'jordan']
def developer_names(devs)
  devs.map do |dev|
    macruby_genius = dev
  end
end
developer_names(developers)
macruby_genius # => "Laurent"
```

In this case, the macruby_genius variable exists in two different contexts. Therefore, even though it is being redefined in each iteration within the developer_names method, the variable set outside of the method is not affected.

Blocks can make your code easier to read and maintain. Let's say you want to create five new Contact instances and add them to an array.

In a different language, you might do something like this:

```
Contact = function(){};
contacts = [];
for (i = 0; i < 5; i++) {
  var contact = new Contact;
  contacts[i] = contact;
}
```

However, with MacRuby, you can just write:

```
# Dummy objects referenced in the example
class Contact; end

# same code as the javascript example above:
contacts = []
5.times do
  contacts << Contact.new
end

# Or you can use this shortened syntax
contacts = Array.new(5){ Contact.new }
```

both of which, at least in my mind, read much better than the version without blocks.

Since MacRuby 0.7.1, Objective-C APIs using C blocks are supported. Here is a simple example using Array#enumerateObjectsUsingBlock (see *http://developer.apple.com/library/ios/documentation/Cocoa/Reference/Foundation/Classes/NSArray_Class/NSArray.html#//apple_ref/doc/uid/20000137-SW19*):

```
framework 'Foundation'
array = [1, 2, 3, 4, 5]
proc = Proc.new do |obj, index, stop|
  p obj
  stop.assign(true) if index == 2
end
array.enumerateObjectsUsingBlock(proc)
```

Here is the output:

```
1
2
3
=> [1, 2, 3, 4, 5]
```

You might be surprised that we changed the value of stop by using #assign. The reason we cannot just use the = operator is that the Objective-C API defines stop as a pointer to a boolean value, so we have to reassign the pointer's value to make the loop stop. Read "Pointers" on page 158 for more information about using pointers with MacRuby.

Concurrency

CPU clock speeds aren't increasing as quickly as they used to. Instead, to scale programs and improve performance, chipset designers have to add more cores to the processors. At the same time, users expect programs to do more complicated things and to do them faster than before.

The obvious solution for a long time was to use threads. The problem with threads is that they require a lot of development attention, and if not handled properly, they can seriously affect the system performance and embed difficult-to-find bugs in programs. Threads are available, and are discussed further in this book. However, since the Snow Leopard release, Apple offers a very interesting API called Grand Central Dispatch (GCD). GCD is an API on top of the libdispatch library (*http://libdispatch.macosforge .org*), which Apple open sourced.

Grand Central Dispatch

MacRuby developers have full access to GCD. Unless you have developed in Objective-C in the past, you probably are not familiar with this library. This section gives you a quick overview of the key APIs. For more information about GCD, refer to Apple's documentation (*http://developer.apple.com/library/ios/#documentation/Performance/ Reference/GCD_libdispatch_Ref/Reference/reference.html*).

Queues

GCD provides and manages *dispatch queues*, which allow developers to execute blocks of code on a pool of threads fully managed by the system (the pool grows and shrinks dynamically and distributes its threads evenly among available processors). You can think of a queue as a pool of workers ready to take orders. You don't have to worry about how they will share the workload among themselves. You pick a queue based on a few key criteria—such as whether they tackle tasks serially or concurrently—and then send the queue instructions about executing your task.

Queues in MacRuby are handled by the `Dispatch::Queue` class. GCD has three types of queues:

Main queue
> Tasks are executed serially on your application's main thread. The main queue is automatically created by the system.

Concurrent queue
> Tasks start executing in the order in which you queue them, but can run concurrently. Use these queues when you want to execute large numbers of tasks concurrently. Three concurrent queues are automatically created for your application: one that runs at a high priority, one that runs at a low priority, and the default queue, which lies between them in priority.

Serial queue

Tasks execute one at a time in first in, first out (FIFO) order. Use this queue type when you want to ensure that tasks are executed in a predictable order. Serial queues have to be created by the programmer.

Queues are interesting for a few reasons, mainly because they are lighter (smaller memory footprint, faster allocation) than threads and because developers can rely on the system to manage them. In practice, this means that instead of worrying about the amount of threads to start and manage, you can start as many queues and tasks as you want and not worry about the nitty-gritty details.

To create a new queue, create an instance of `Dispatch::Queue` and give it a name:

```
queue = Dispatch::Queue.new('com.oreilly.guide')
```

 The default dispatch queues are serial queues. You can create as many serial queues as you want, and they will run in parallel with each other. But if you want to execute many tasks at the same time, it is more efficient to use a concurrent queue.

Once you have a queue instance, you can dispatch tasks to it using Ruby blocks (see the section "Blocks" on page 137 as a reminder). Tasks can be dispatched synchronously or asynchronously, as shown here:

```
queue = Dispatch::Queue.new('com.oreilly.guide')
queue.sync do
  puts 'Blocking operation...'
  sleep(3)
  puts 'done waiting!'
end
puts 'Synchronous dispatching evaluated'

queue.async do
  puts "Async call..."
  sleep(3)
  puts 'Async block done'
end
puts 'Asynchronous dispatching evaluated'
```

If you run this code, you will notice that the first call using #sync is a blocking call and the rest of the code won't be executed until after the block is done running. The other call, using #async, isn't blocking and will be executed concurrently because it is being processed in the background.

Using the synchronous approach ensures the data is accessed by only one task at a time, making the use of a mutex redundant while keeping the code simple. Here is an implementation example showing how a missing launcher class can ensure its instances fire in the proper order, one after the other, respecting the chronological order:

```
class MissileLauncher
  def initialize
    @queue = Dispatch::Queue.new('org.macruby.synchronizer')
  end
  def launch!
    # Because serial queues execute their tasks in FIFO order, we can be sure
    # that only one thread will be running the passed block at any given time.
    @queue.sync do
      # critical section: here we arm the missiles and fire them.
      puts "BOOM!"
    end
  end
end
```

If you don't need to run your tasks in a given order, you can use the concurrent queues:

```
Dispatch::Queue.concurrent(:default).async do
  # expensive calculation run concurrently
end
# which is the same as
Dispatch::Queue.concurrent.async do
  # expensive calculation run concurrently
end
# Other concurrent queues can be used calling them using
# their priority level:
Dispatch::Queue.concurrent(:low)
Dispatch::Queue.concurrent(:high)
```

 The main queue isn't covered in detail here, since it's not useful for concurrency. However, it should never be used for long-running tasks, because it keeps the UI from interacting with the user.

Groups

GCD groups are designed to make task synchronization trivial. In some cases, you need to ensure a queue has executed all of its tasks before doing something else. After you create a group, you can assign tasks to it as you dispatch them and make your code wait for all the group's tasks to be executed. Alternatively, you can register a block to be triggered when the group's tasks have all executed.

Here is the MacRuby implementation of the concept of Futures, found in the Io language (*http://www.iolanguage.com/*). Basically, the concept is simple: create a proxy object performing expensive computations in the background and then collect the results:

```
class Future
  def initialize(&block)
    # Each thread gets its own FIFO queue upon which we will dispatch
    # the delayed computation passed in the &block variable.
    Thread.current[:futures] ||=
      Dispatch::Queue.new("org.macruby.futures-#{Thread.current.object_id}")
    @group = Dispatch::Group.new
```

```
    # Asynchronously dispatch the future to the thread-local queue.
    Thread.current[:futures].async(@group) { @value = block.call }
  end
  def value
    # Wait for the computation to finish (if not already done)
    @group.wait
    # then just return the value in question.
    @value
  end
end
```

Use the following to create a future and fetch the result of the calculation:

```
result = Future.new do
  p 'Engaging delayed computation!'
  sleep 2.5
  42 # Your result would go here.
end

# Then to fetch the calculation result:
result.value # => 42
```

The important aspect of this implementation is that we are defining a queue and a group. We are then dispatching blocks to the group. Before checking the value, we are first verifying that all the tasks have executed. It's common practice to group concurrent tasks inside a serial queue to process groups of tasks in a sequential order.

The following example shows how to speed up `Array#map` by spreading out the total work across the system's available processors:

```
class Array
  def parallel_map(&block)
    result = []
    # Creating a group to synchronize block execution.
    group = Dispatch::Group.new
    # We will access the `result` array from within this serial queue,
    # as without a GIL (Global Interpreter Lock) we cannot assume array access
    # to be thread-safe.
    result_queue = Dispatch::Queue.new('access-queue.#{result.object_id}')
    0.upto(self.size) do |idx|
      # Dispatch a task to the default concurrent queue.
      Dispatch::Queue.concurrent.async(group) do
        temp = block[self[idx]]
        result_queue.async(group) { result[idx] = temp }
      end
    end
    # Wait for all the blocks to finish.
    group.wait
    result
  end
end
```

MacRuby doesn't use a Global Interpreter Lock (a lock preventing multiple threads to access the same data at the same time), which means that it is truly concurrent. You can read more about Ruby and concurrency in an article from my blog at *http://merbist.com/2011/02/22/con currency-in-ruby-explained.*

GCD also offers other features, such as interthread communication and resource management, as well as a low-level foundation for event-based programming. But these features fall outside of the scope of this section.

GCD dispatch gem

While MacRuby has native full access to the GCD APIs, in some cases, developers might wish to use more abstraction and get some extra features. This is what the GCD dispatch gem offers.

Like all Ruby gems, the dispatch gem (*http://rubygems.org/gems/dispatch*) is hosted on Rubygems.org.

To install the gem, enter the following:

```
$ macgem install dispatch
```

 MacRuby lets you bundle gems with your apps when you compile it.

Here is a quick tour of what is available to you:

```
require 'dispatch'
job = Dispatch::Job.new { slow_operation }
job.value # => "wait for the result"
```

As you can see, the API looks very similar to the Thread API. The difference is that the "Dispatch::Job" is in reality a wrapper around GCD's default concurrent queue. When you add a new block to the queue, the main thread doesn't stall.

To retrieve the result of the passed block, you have two options. The one shown above, calling #value on a job, will block the current thread until the job is processed. The other option is to use the asynchronous API, as follows:

```
require 'dispatch'
job = Dispatch::Job.new { slow_operation }
job.value do |v|
  "operation result: #{v} - asynchronous dispatched!"
end
```

In this case, the result of the job processing will be triggered asynchronously and the result will be passed to the block.

But that's not all. You can send a bunch of operations to a job and let GCD decide how many threads should be used underneath—all of that is totally transparent to you:

```
require 'dispatch'
job = Dispatch::Job.new
job.add { slow_operation(a) }
job.add { slow_operation(b) }
job.add { slow_operation(c) }
job.join
job.values # =>[result_a, result_b, result_c]
```

Calling values in this case returns all the returned operation results. However, this is not a blocking call, so to make sure all the operations are done processing, the caller calls #join.

The only challenge with this approach is that because in MacRuby each thread runs in its own nonlocking, reentrant VM, there is a risk of destroying data integrity. Two operations might try to access the same data at the same time, corrupting the data.

Luckily, MacRuby comes with another wrapper around GCD's serial queues, providing lock-free synchronization. Simply speaking, the developer defines a proxy object that has a private access queue, making sure it keeps its data integrity:

```
require 'dispatch'
job = Dispatch::Job.new
@scores = job.synchronize Hash.new
[user1, user2, user3].each do |user|
  job.add{ @scores[user.name] = calculate(user) }
end
job.join
@scores[user1.name] # => 1042
@scores[user2.name] # => 673
@scores[user3.name] # => 845
```

MacRuby's wrapper even goes further and provides a concurrent alternative version of most of the Ruby enumerable methods. What I mean by that is that by using the parallel version of an enumerable method, we let GCD run each iteration concurrently. Consider the following code:

```
start = Time.now
25.times do
  sleep(1)
end
puts "Took #{Time.now - start} seconds"
# => Took 25.011652 seconds
```

As expected, the code took a bit more than 25 seconds, since we asked it to sleep 25 times for 1 second.

Now, let's use the concurrent version provided by GCD:

```
require 'dispatch'
start = Time.now
25.p_times do
  sleep(1)
```

```
  end
  puts "Took #{Time.now - start} seconds"
  # => Took 13.028822 seconds
```

Instead of calling #times, we called #p_times, which is the parallel/concurrent version of #times. In the background, GCD figures out the optimal number of threads to use and runs the iterations in parallel.

This example should let you imagine how you can optimize the performance of your code by running your iterations in parallel:

```
require 'dispatch'
locations = ["San Diego", "Chicago", "New Orleans", "Paris", "Singapore"]
locations.p_each do |location|
  # expensive calculation
  location.update_stats
end
```

 The concurrent enumerable methods are synchronous, meaning they won't return until all the iterations have completed. This way, the APIs stay close to their nonconcurrent counterparts.

To see the available concurrent enumerable methods you can use this trick:

```
$ macruby -rdispatch -e "puts [].methods.grep(/^p_/)"
# => p_each
# => p_each_with_index
# => p_map
# => p_mapreduce
# => p_find_all
# => p_find
```

To get the list, I just asked MacRuby to evaluate a string after requiring the dispatch library. Call the macruby binary with the --help flag to see the various options. Because we checked on the enumerable methods, p_times wasn't displayed, because it is defined on the Integer class.

The last GCD wrapper feature that I would like to introduce is the MapReduce implementation (see the Wikipedia entry for MapReduce at *http://en.wikipedia.org/wiki/ MapReduce*). MapReduce allows you to process large amounts of data in parallel and compute the results. Let's look at some examples to understand better the usefulness of this concept:

```
require 'dispatch'
map_reduce = (0..1_000_000).p_mapreduce(0){|n| Math.sqrt(n)}
map_reduce # => 666667166.393145
```

This example iterates through all numbers from 0 to one million, calculates the square root of each, and ends up by adding all the results together. The addition is implicit and you can specify another operator if you wish to do so.

Ruby developers might see a similarity with the #inject method, except that in p_map reduce, you have to define a starting value (0 in this example):

```ruby
require 'dispatch'
map_reduce = (0..10_000).p_mapreduce([], :<<) do |n|
  Math.sqrt(n)
end
```

This code is the same as the following, except that the following runs iterations consecutively instead of concurrently:

```ruby
map_reduce = (0..10_000).inject([]) do |sum, n|
  sum << Math.sqrt(n)
end
```

Code parallelization is difficult, and merely running iterations concurrently doesn't necessarily mean you will see better results. One of the rules of parallelization is to parallelize only costly code. As a matter of fact, based on that recommendation, the square root examples shown earlier don't make a lot of sense. Let's write a real example and see what kind of performance improvement GCD has to offer on my two-core machine:

```ruby
require 'benchmark'

# Monte Carlo method to find an estimated version of Pi
# For more info, read: http://en.wikipedia.org/wiki/Monte_Carlo_method
def estimated_pi(repetitions)
  inside = 0
  repetitions.times do
    inside += 1 if (Math.sqrt(rand**2+rand**2) < 1)
  end
  ((4*inside))/repetitions.to_f
end

n = 50_000
Benchmark.bm(7) do |x|
  x.report("times:")   { n.times do estimated_pi(200) end }
  x.report("p_times:") { n.p_times do estimated_pi(200) end }
end
```

This code generates the following output:

```
            user     system     total       real
times:    6.030000  0.010000  6.040000 (  6.149780)
p_times:  6.300000  0.020000  6.320000 (  3.576102)
```

Technically, the code takes the same amount of time to execute when you use #times and when you use #p_times. The user, system, and total times are therefore pretty similar, and in fact, the system time for the parallel version is worse (probably because of the overhead of task management). However, the real time reported is half the duration when using the concurrent method. Because the iterations run in parallel on the two cores, the same amount of code can be processed much faster.

GCD offers many more low-level features, such as custom queues, semaphores, and asynchronous events based on sources (timers, signals, and file descriptors, which can be files or sockets). More information is available in the wrapper's readme file (*http://github.com/MacRuby/MacRuby/tree/trunk/lib/dispatch*).

Sandboxing

OS X ships with a security facility called sandbox (*http://developer.apple.com/library/mac/#documentation/Darwin/Reference/ManPages/man7/sandbox.7.html*). Sandbox restricts a process's access to resources. For instance, you can sandbox your application so it doesn't access the Internet or the local network, or can't read or write to disk. The sandboxing applies to your entire application, including C extensions or Cocoa APIs you might be using. By using the sandbox facility in your application, you limit potential damage that can happen if a vulnerability in your application is exploited.

MacRuby exposes the `Sandbox` class to make easy use of the facility. The class comes with five sandboxing profiles:

`Sandbox.pure_computation`
> All operating system services are prohibited.

`Sandbox.no_internet`
> TCP/IP networking is prohibited.

`Sandbox.no_network`
> All socket-based networking is prohibited.

`Sandbox.temporary_writes`
> File system writes are restricted to temporary folders.

`Sandbox.no_writes`
> File system writes are prohibited.

You can also define your own profiles and load them. Check the API for more information.

To apply a sandbox profile, you just need to call `#apply!` on the profile. Here is an example:

```
require 'open-uri'
begin
  Sandbox.no_internet.apply!
  open('http://www.macruby.org')
rescue SystemCallError => exception
  puts exception
end
```

If you execute the preceding code, you will get the following output: `Operation not permitted - connect(2)`.

If you acquire resources before initiating the sandbox, these resources won't be controlled by the sandbox.

Using Objective-C or C Code

Because MacRuby runs inside the Objective-C runtime, you can directly call Objective-C and C code using the Ruby syntax. However, some API symbols of frameworks or libraries cannot be introspected at runtime, usually because they are ANSI C symbols denoting nonobject-oriented items such as constants, enumerations, structures, and functions. Apple has provided Objective-C bridges and languages with a way to access these symbols nonetheless. This tool is called the Objective-C Bridges Metadata Generator (*http://bridgesupport.macosforge.org*), or BridgeSupport for short. Apple started shipping BridgeSupport in Mac OS 10.5 Leopard. The project is open source and you can download the latest version or the source code directly from macosforge.org.

BridgeSupport comes with pregenerated files for all system frameworks. However, the version shipped before Mac OS 10.7 Lion had some bugs. It's recommended that you use the latest version of BridgeSupport and embed newly generated files with your project.

BridgeSupport comes with XML files describing the C symbols for the system frameworks. But what if you want to use your own Objective-C/C code or a third-party framework or library? It's actually very simple. BridgeSupport ships with a command-line tool that allows you to create XML files for your symbols.

Let's pretend I would like to use a framework called FooBar and that this framework uses constants, so I can't access them from MacRuby directly. The easiest way to make the framework compatible is to generate a BridgeSupport file and to add it to the framework as follows:

```
$ gen_bridge_metadata --64-bit -f ~/Desktop/FooBar.framework/
    -o ~/Desktop/FooBar.framework/Resources/BridgeSupport/FooBar.bridgesupport
```

You can see all the options by entering the following:

```
$ gen_bridge_metadata --help
```

In this example, we use the `--64-bit` flag to generate 64-bit annotations and the `-f` (framework) flag to specify that we are generating a support file for a framework. Finally, we use the `-o` (output) flag to save the file directly in the framework.

The BridgeSupport folder might not exist inside your framework. No big deal—just make sure to create it before generating the support file:

```
$ mkdir -p ~/Desktop/FooBar.framework/Resources/BridgeSupport
```

A BridgeSupport can be installed in one of the following locations:

- /Library/Frameworks/MyFramework/Resources/BridgeSupport
- /Library/BridgeSupport
- ~/Library/BridgeSupport
- /System/Library/BridgeSupport

For more information about BridgeSupport, check out the manual page by entering the following:

```
$ man gen_bridge_metadata
```

 Ruby methods starting with an uppercase letter must be called with explicit parentheses so they don't get confused with a constant. C functions usually start with an uppercase letter, and therefore you need to make sure to use parentheses even if no arguments are needed.

Scriptable Applications

Mac OS X version 10.5 and later ship with a framework called Scripting Bridge. This framework allows developers to communicate with scriptable applications directly from within their code. Before Mac OS X version 10.5, developers had to use Apple-Script scripts to send and handle Apple events. Using this new framework, MacRuby developers can interact directly with applications such as iChat, iTunes, iPhoto, iCal, Keynote, and so on.

A OS X application is said to be scriptable when it exposes a dictionary of Apple events. These events are hooks into the application. The easiest way to see which applications are scriptable and what APIs they expose is to use the AppleScript Editor application. Open AppleScript Editor and click File → Open Dictionary. Choose iTunes and browse the API (Figure 8-1).

OS X also has a series of command-line tools to inspect scriptable applications and show the available methods. The primary tool is called sdef (scripting definition extractor), which extracts the scripting definition of an application. You can give it a try in your terminal by entering the following:

```
$ /usr/bin/sdef /Applications/iTunes.app
```

The result is a long XML file describing an Apple event dictionary. The challenge is that some of these definitions use nonobject-oriented items such as constants and enumerations. So what you need to do next is create a BridgeSupport file ("Using Objective-C or C Code" on page 149) to make sure you can use the full API from MacRuby.

 These steps are not necessary if the API doesn't use nonobject-oriented items, but to be safe, we are still going through the entire process.

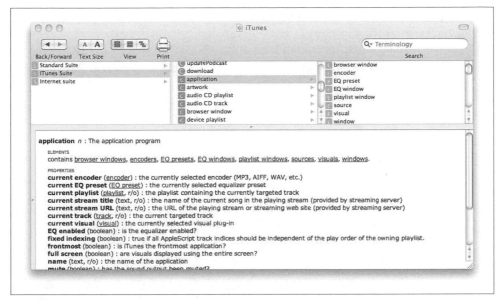

Figure 8-1. The AppleScript Editor

To create a BridgeSupport file, use the `sdp` command. `sdp` is an sdef processor:

```
$ sdef /Applications/iTunes.app | sdp -fh --basename iTunes
```

`sdef`, `sdp`, `gen_bridge_metadata`, and other tools are located in */usr/bin*, which should be in your path.

The previous command generates a scripting definition for iTunes and pipes it to the scripting processor. The processor generates a Scripting Bridge Objective-C header and sets the base name of the generated header file to *iTunes*. The result is a file called *iTunes.h* that we can convert into a BridgeSupport file using `gen_bridge_metadata`:

```
$ gen_bridge_metadata -c '-I.' iTunes.h > iTunes.bridgesupport
```

Now we have a BridgeSupport file and are ready to start playing with the Scripting Bridge framework to control iTunes. Turn off iTunes, write the following code in a file, and execute it from the command line:

```
framework 'Foundation'
framework 'ScriptingBridge'

itunes = SBApplication.applicationWithBundleIdentifier("com.apple.itunes")
load_bridge_support_file 'iTunes.bridgesupport'
itunes.run
itunes.playpause
```

If everything goes well, iTunes is initialized and starts playing.

At home, I have a MacMini in my living room. In my bedroom, I set up a pair of speakers connected via an AirPort Express. What's nice with this setup is that I can stream music from my MacMini to my speakers and even control what music is played via my iPhone.

Using MacRuby, I decided to write a small script that would start iTunes and play a special playlist every morning to wake me up slowly. Here is the script in question:

```
#!/usr/local/bin/macruby
framework 'Foundation'
framework 'ScriptingBridge'

itunes = SBApplication.applicationWithBundleIdentifier("com.apple.itunes")
load_bridge_support_file 'iTunes.bridgesupport'
itunes.run
itunes.stop
library = itunes.sources.find{|source| source.name == 'Library'}
playlist = library.userPlaylists.find do |playlist|
  playlist.name == 'morning'
end
playlist.playOnce(false) if playlist
```

The script is pretty straightforward. After starting iTunes (if it is not already started) and stopping any item already playing, the script finds the music library and then finds the playlist named *morning*. If the playlist is found, it is then played.

The AppleScript Editor doesn't always show all the different available methods, and the documentation might not reflect the options you need. The best way to introspect the available classes is to read the header file or use the interactive command:

```
$ macirb --simple-prompt
>> framework 'Foundation'
=> true
>> framework 'ScriptingBridge'
=> true
>> itunes = SBApplication.applicationWithBundleIdentifier("com.apple.itunes")
=> #<ITunesApplication:0x200c5bce0>
> (itunes.methods(true, true) - Object.new.methods(true, true)).sort
=> [:EQEnabled, :EQPresets, :EQWindows, :activate, :"add:to:", :backTrack,
 :browserWindows, :"childWithClass:code:keyForm:keyData:",
 :"childWithClass:code:keyForm:keyData:length:type:",
 :"childWithClass:code:keyForm:keyData:type:",
 :"childWithClass:code:keyForm:keyData:keyDesc:",
 :classForScriptingClass, :classNamesForCodes, :classesForScriptingNames,
 :codesForPropertyNames, :context, :convert, :currentEQPreset,
 :currentEncoder, :currentPlaylist, :currentStreamTitle, :currentStreamURL,
 :currentTrack, :currentVisual, :delegate, :descriptionForSpecifier,
 :eject, :elementArrayWithCode, :"elementWithCode:ID:",
 :"elementWithCode:atIndex:", :"elementWithCode:named:", :encodeWithCoder,
 :encoders, :fastForward, :fixedIndexing, :frontmost, :fullScreen, :get,
 :"initWithApplication:specifier:", :initWithBundleIdentifier,
 :"initWithClass:properties:data:", :initWithCoder, :initWithContext,
 :"initWithContext:specifier:", :initWithData,
 :"initWithElementCode:properties:data:", :initWithProcessIdentifier,
 :initWithProperties, :initWithURL, :isRangeSpecifier, :isRunning,
 :lastError, :launchFlags, :mute, :name, :nextTrack, :openLocation, :pause,
```

```
  :"play:once:", :playerPosition, :playerState, :playlistWindows,
  :playpause, :positionAfter, :positionBefore, :previousTrack,
  :"print:printDialog:withProperties:kind:theme:", :properties,
  :"propertyWithClass:code:", :propertyWithCode, :qualifiedSpecifier,
  :qualify, :quit, :resume, :rewind, :run, :selection,
  :"sendEvent:id:format:", :"sendEvent:id:parameters:", :sendMode,
  :setCurrentEQPreset, :setCurrentEncoder, :setCurrentVisual, :setDelegate,
  :setEQEnabled, :setFixedIndexing, :setFrontmost, :setFullScreen,
  :setLastError, :setLaunchFlags, :setMute, :setPlayerPosition,
  :setSendMode, :setSoundVolume, :setTimeout, :setTo, :setVisualSize,
  :setVisualsEnabled, :shouldCreateClasses, :soundVolume, :sources,
  :specifier, :specifierDescription, :stop, :subscribe, :timeout, :update,
  :updateAllPodcasts, :updatePodcast, :version, :visualSize, :visuals,
  :visualsEnabled, :windows]
>> itunes.methods(true, true).grep(/play/)
=> [:playpause, :"play:once:", :playerState, :playerPosition, :playlistWindows]
```

Method Missing

Method missing is a generic Ruby approach to catching undefined method calls and executing some code based on the undefined method name.

This is a very handy solution to wrap cumbersome Cocoa APIs. It allows you to pick out Cocoa classes you use often and create a more Ruby-like API for them. Let's take, for example, the AddressBook framework. (see *http://developer.apple.com/mac/library/ documentation/UserExperience/Conceptual/AddressBook/AddressBook.html*). This is an old framework that might not seem very natural at first. Here is a simple example:

```
framework 'AddressBook'
first_contact = ABAddressBook.sharedAddressBook.people.first
puts first_contact.valueForProperty(kABOrganizationProperty)
=> "Apple Inc."
```

The code above is pretty straightforward: it loads the AddressBook framework and uses the ABAddressBook class method called sharedAddressBook to fetch an address book. It then calls the people method on the book, taking only the first person from the array that is returned (#first in Ruby is equivalent to [0]). Of course, before calling this code, I had to dig around in the documentation.

The odd API part is how you access a contact's property. The Framework expects you to call #valueForProperty on your contact and to pass it a constant that defines the property type. By introspecting first_contact, we find that it's an instance of the ABPerson class.

The *ABPerson C Reference* documentation lists all the properties available and the associated constants:

```
CFStringRef kABFirstNameProperty;
CFStringRef kABLastNameProperty;
CFStringRef kABFirstNamePhoneticProperty;
CFStringRef kABLastNamePhoneticProperty;
CFStringRef kABBirthdayProperty;
```

```
CFStringRef kABOrganizationProperty;
CFStringRef kABJobTitleProperty;
CFStringRef kABHomePageProperty;
CFStringRef kABURLsProperty;
CFStringRef kABCalendarURIsProperty;
CFStringRef kABEmailProperty;
CFStringRef kABAddressProperty;
CFStringRef kABPhoneProperty;
CFStringRef kABAIMInstantProperty;
CFStringRef kABJabberInstantProperty;
CFStringRef kABMSNInstantProperty;
CFStringRef kABYahooInstantProperty;
CFStringRef kABICQInstantProperty;
CFStringRef kABNoteProperty;
CFStringRef kABMiddleNameProperty;
CFStringRef kABMiddleNamePhoneticProperty;
CFStringRef kABTitleProperty;
CFStringRef kABSuffixProperty;
CFStringRef kABNicknameProperty;
CFStringRef kABMaidenNameProperty;
CFStringRef kABOtherDatesProperty;
CFStringRef kABRelatedNamesProperty;
CFStringRef kABDepartmentProperty;
CFStringRef kABPersonFlags;
```

 In Objective-C, a constant can start with a lowercase character, but in MacRuby, constants always have to start with an uppercase character. So, for instance, if you want to use the kABFirstNameProperty constant, you have to use the KABFirstNameProperty constant in MacRuby.

Method missing allows us to define a different, potentially nicer API without having to define a method for each constant. Here is what the API will look like:

```
first_contact.organization # Acme Inc.
first_contact.first_name # Giana
first_contact.last_name # Aimonetti
```

And here is the implementation:

```
class ABPerson

  def method_missing(m, *args, &block)
    segments = m.to_s.split('_')
    missing_meth = segments.map{|part| part.capitalize}.join
    constant_name = "KAB#{missing_meth}Property"
    if Object.const_defined?(constant_name)
      self.valueForProperty Object.const_get(constant_name)
    else
      super
    end
  end

end
```

This might seem quite cryptic if you are new to Ruby and metaprogramming. Basically, we are reopening the ABPerson class and defining a method_missing method to catch our new calls. method_missing takes three arguments: the name of the method (m) as a symbol, an array of arguments (*args), and a block. In our case, our implementation converts the method passed (FirstNameProperty, for instance) to the format expected for a constant (KABFirstNameProperty). If the constant exists, the method dispatches the call using #valueForProperty and passing the constant. Otherwise, we let MacRuby raise an exception.

In this section, we will examine how to implement method missing and how it works so you can also wrap some unneeded complexity in a nice and clean API.

The following method_missing method is defined for Cocoa's NSSpeechSynthesizer API:

```ruby
framework 'AppKit'
class Greeter
  attr_reader :user

  def initialize(commands = {})
    voice_type  = "com.apple.speech.synthesis.voice.Vicki"
    @voice      = NSSpeechSynthesizer.alloc.initWithVoice(voice_type)
    @user       = NSUserName()
    @commands   = {:hello => "Hello there #{user}, how are you today?",
                   :bye   => "Adios #{user}, come back soon!"}.merge(commands)
  end

  def method_missing(meth_symbol, *args, &block)
    command = @commands[meth_symbol]
    if command
      message = command.respond_to?(:call) ? command.call(self) : command
      @voice.startSpeakingString(message)
    end
  end
end
```

Open a new *macirb* session and copy/paste the previous code, or save it in a file and require it from *macirb*. You can then run a speech synthesizer session as follows:

```
$ macirb --simple-prompt
>> require 'method_missing_example'
=> true
>> vicki = Greeter.new
>> vicki.respond_to?(:hello)
=> false
>> vicki.hello
=> true
# greetings message is played
```

As you can see, we were able to call a method that doesn't exist (hello), thanks to method_missing.

For those not used to reading Ruby code, attr_reader :user is the equivalent of a getter for the instance variable @user, making it available via the user instance method. Our initializer takes an optional argument called commands, which defaults to an empty

Hash if not passed. The `commands` local variable is then merged with a list of default commands. This way, we can pass additional commands when creating our `Greeter` instance.

Finally, in the `method_missing` method body, we are checking whether the command object responds to the `call` method. If it does, we send the `call` method to it and save the result in the local variable `message`. Otherwise, we just use the `command` value (we do that so a command can be defined as an anonymous method). The message is then read by our `@voice` object.

Let's see whether passing a new command when creating a new greeter does what we expect:

```
>> vicki2 = Greeter.new(:howdy => "Howdy cowboy?")
>> vicki2.howdy
# sound of the new greeting defined on the fly.
```

Now let's do something a bit more tricky and pass an anonymous method that needs to be executed every single time it's called:

```
>> time_cmd = Proc.new{"It's #{Time.new.hour}, #{Time.new.min} and
>> #{Time.now.sec} seconds"}
>> vicki3 = Greeter.new(:time => time_cmd)
>> vicki3.time
# check that the seconds changed
>> vicki3.time
# time changed
```

Finally, let's look at a way of optimizing the performance of our code by using some more metaprogramming. This time, we are going to define methods dynamically at runtime. Instead of always looking up the command and dynamically telling the voice what to say, once a missing method is called, we can add a new method into the class so that we never call the same missing method twice:

```
framework 'AppKit'
class Greeter
  attr_reader :user

  def initialize(commands = {})
    voice_type = "com.apple.speech.synthesis.voice.Vicki"
    @voice     = NSSpeechSynthesizer.alloc.initWithVoice(voice_type)
    @user      = NSUserName()
    @commands  = {:hello => "Hello there #{user}, how are you today?",
                  :bye   => "Adios #{user}, come back soon!"}.merge(commands)
  end

  def method_missing(meth_symbol, *args, &block)
    command = @commands[meth_symbol]
    if command
      self.class.send(:define_method, meth_symbol.to_s) do
        message = command.respond_to?(:call) ? command.call(self) : command
        @voice.startSpeakingString(message)
      end
      # call the newly defined method
```

```
          send(meth_symbol)
        end
      end
    end

$ macirb --simple-prompt
>> require 'method_missing_example'
>> vicki = Greeter.new
>> vicki.respond_to?(:bye)
=> false
>> vicki.bye
>> vicki.respond_to?(:bye)
=> true
```

To optimize this code, we use some Ruby tricks you might not be aware of. The "magic" happens inside the method_missing method implementation. We already talked about method_missing, but we haven't talked about send and define_method. To illustrate the power of these methods, I'll explain quickly what the code example does:

```
def method_missing(meth_symbol, *args, &block)
  command = @commands[meth_symbol]
  if command
    self.class.send(:define_method, meth_symbol.to_s) do
      message = command.respond_to?(:call) ? command.call(self) : command
      @voice.startSpeakingString(message)
    end
    # call the newly defined method
    send(meth_symbol)
  end
end
```

The first thing we do is check that the missing method matches a defined command. If it does, we define the method on the fly. For that, we define the missing method on the class itself. We can't call the define_method directly on the class, because define_method is a private method and you can't call a private method from outside of the object. So, instead, we use the send method. The send method is a way to dynamically dispatch a method by using its name as a string or a symbol. Using send, we can call define_method on the class and pass the missing method name as an argument. The block passed to define_method will become the new method's body. Once the method is defined, we call it using send again and pass it the method name as a symbol. There is a lot going on in just a few lines of code—take some time to experiment on your own.

As you can see, after calling the bye method a first time, the method becomes defined and the Greeter instance knows that it can respond to it.

Method missing is a very powerful tool and, like most metaprogramming tricks, needs to be used with care. Read more on Ruby metaprogramming to see all the interesting possibilities that are available to you.

Pointers

In the block example earlier in this chapter, we discussed that when using Objective-C or C APIs we might have to deal with pointers. MacRuby exposes a Pointer object that allows you to allocate memory of a given type to a given number of elements. To create a pointer to a float value, for instance, you can choose one of the two constructor options:

```
pointer = Pointer.new(:float)
# or
pointer = Pointer.new_with_type(:f)
```

Table 8-1 shows available data types. The list can also be found on Apple's website (see *http://developer.apple.com/library/mac/#documentation/Cocoa/Conceptual/ObjCRuntimeGuide/Introduction/Introduction.html*).

Table 8-1. Available data types

Pointer code	Pointer type	Constructor example
c	char	Pointer.new(:char)
*	char string	Pointer.new(:string)
i	int	Pointer.new(:integer)
s	short	Pointer.new(:short)
l	long	Pointer.new(:long)
C	unsigned char	Pointer.new(:uchar)
I	unsigned integer	Pointer.new(:uint)
S	unsigned short	Pointer.new(:ushort)
L	unsigned long	Pointer.new(:ulong)
f	float	Pointer.new(:float)
@	object	Pointer.new(:object) or Pointer.new(:id)
B	Boolean	Pointer.new(:boolean)
#	class	Pointer.new(:class)
:	selector	Pointer.new(:selector)

You can create pointers by passing the symbol name as shown above, and also by passing the pointer type code as a string.

You can dereference the pointer the same way you access an array in Ruby.

You can also have a pointer to multiple values. Here is how you create a pointer with bounds:

```
pointer = Pointer.new(:float, 4)
pointer[0] = 1.0
pointer[1] = 2.0
pointer[2] = 3.0
pointer[3] = 4.0
pointer[0] # => 1.0
pointer[1] # => 2.0
pointer[2] # => 3.0
pointer[3] # => 4.0
```

To assign a value to the pointer, you can use one of these two methods:

```
pointer.assign(3.2)
# or
pointer[0]= 3.2
```

When you use [ ] and [ ]=, you must be careful not to try to access or set a value out of bounds. Unfortunately, there is no way to find out a pointer's bounds.

Dereferencing pointers is pretty straightforward and was shown earlier:

```
pointer = Pointer.new(:integer)
pointer.assign(42)
pointer[0] # => 42
```

You can also offset pointers using the + and the - methods:

```
pointer = Pointer.new(:long, 10)
10.times{|i| pointer[i] = i }
pointer2 = pointer + 2
pointer2[0] # => 2
pointer2[1] # => 3
pointer2[2] # => 4
```

One situation that requires offsetting is when you are using a read method that accepts a pointer of bytes and returns the number of bytes actually read. You can set a pointer, pass it to the method, offset it, and pass it again. Here is a dummy example of such an API:

```
ptr = dataOut;
fakeAPI(dataIn, dataInLength, ptr, dataOutAvailable
        &dataOutMoved);
ptr += dataOutMoved;
dataOutAvailable -= dataOutMoved;
otherAPI(ptr, dataOutAvailable, &dataOutMoved);
```

Two types of Objective-C pointers are not directly supported by MacRuby: void pointers and unknown type pointers (also called unsigned pointers). Let's look at how to work with these types.

Void Pointers

Most methods in APIs based on CoreFoundation use pointers to CFTypeRefs, which technically are pointers to void (also known as void *). If a method expects a void pointer argument, you can pass a pointer of any type.

Let's look at an example from the Accessibility API:

```
extern AXError AXUIElementCopyAttributeValue (
        AXUIElementRef element,
        CFStringRef attribute,
        CFTypeRef *value);
```

As you can see, this is a C function that takes a pointer as its last argument. The reason for using a pointer is that it will hold the function result after it's called and the caller can retrieve the result from the pointer. The notable issue with this function is that, as mentioned, it returns the retrieved data in the final parameter (value), and therefore requires a pointer as that parameter. To use the method in MacRuby, create a variable (here named titlePtr) and assign it to an object pointer. Pass the pointer value to the function and read the retrieved value just by dereferencing it, as shown here:

```
framework 'ApplicationServices'
pid = 433
safari = AXUIElementCreateApplication(pid)
titlePtr = Pointer.new(:id)
err = AXUIElementCopyAttributeValue(safari, "AXTitle", titlePtr)
p titlePtr[0] # => "Safari"
```

Unsigned Pointer

Some methods take unsigned pointers, that is, pointers that don't have a defined type. Take the FSevents API (see *http://developer.apple.com/library/mac/#documentation/ Darwin/Conceptual/FSEvents_ProgGuide/UsingtheFSEventsFramework/UsingtheFSE ventsFramework.html*), for instance.

Here is a MacRuby script that implements this method to watch a specific folder:

```
callback = Proc.new do |stream, client_callback_info, number_of_events,
                        paths_pointer, event_flags, event_ids|
  puts paths_pointer[0] # => 0
end

paths = [File.expand_path('~/tmp')]
stream = FSEventStreamCreate(KCFAllocatorDefault, callback, nil, paths,
                            KFSEventStreamEventIdSinceNow, 0.0, 0)
FSEventStreamScheduleWithRunLoop(stream, CFRunLoopGetCurrent(), KCFRunLoopDefaultMode)
FSEventStreamStart(stream)

NSRunLoop.currentRunLoop.runUntilDate(NSDate.distantFuture)
```

If you run this code and modify or create a file in *~/tmp*, the callback will be triggered, but the output will be 0. You can see why by looking at the callback function's signature (see *http://developer.apple.com/library/mac/documentation/Darwin/Reference/FSE vents_Ref/FSEvents_h/index.html//apple_ref/c/tdef/FSEventStreamCallback*):

```
void mycallback(
    ConstFSEventStreamRef streamRef,
    void *clientCallBackInfo,
    size_t numEvents,
```

```
        void *eventPaths,
        const FSEventStreamEventFlags eventFlags[],
        const FSEventStreamEventId eventIds[])
    { }
```

eventPaths is a void pointer and therefore can't be properly cast by MacRuby. In a case like this, you need to tell MacRuby how to cast the pointer using the #cast! method:

```
callback = Proc.new do |stream, client_callback_info, number_of_events,
                        paths_pointer, event_flags, event_ids|
  paths_pointer.cast!("*") # cast as a string pointer
  puts paths_pointer[0] # => /Users/mattetti/tmp/
end

paths = [File.expand_path('~/tmp')]
stream = FSEventStreamCreate(KCFAllocatorDefault, callback, nil, paths,
                        KFSEventStreamEventIdSinceNow, 0.0, 0)
FSEventStreamScheduleWithRunLoop(stream, CFRunLoopGetCurrent(), KCFRunLoopDefaultMode)
FSEventStreamStart(stream)

NSRunLoop.currentRunLoop.runUntilDate(NSDate.distantFuture)
```

Some methods optionally take integers in void * parameters. An example is OpenGL's glVertexPointer function, which, when overloaded, takes an integer passed as the last void * pointer. To do that in MacRuby, you need to create a special pointer type using the Pointer#magic_cookie method, and pass it the integer to use.

This is how you call the function in C:

```
glVertexPointer(3, GL_FLOAT, 3, (void *) 12)
```

Using MacRuby you call it this way:

```
glVertexPointer(3, GL_FLOAT, 3, Pointer.magic_cookie(13))
```

Finally, the last edge case with void pointers is when an API returns a direct reference to an object. You can't therefore cast the MacRuby pointer instance value, but should cast the pointer instance itself. Do this via the Pointer's instance method called to_object.

Here is an example using the C-based Text Input Source Services from the HIToolbox framework. Use the TISGetInputSourceProperty function to get the value of a specified input source (see *http://developer.apple.com/library/mac/#documentation/TextFonts/ Reference/TextInputSourcesReference/Reference/reference.html*).

Here is the function signature:

```
void* TISGetInputSourceProperty (
    TISInputSourceRef inputSource,
    CFStringRef propertyKey
);
```

This is how to use it to get the localized name of the current keyboard:

```
framework 'Cocoa'

keyboard = TISCopyCurrentKeyboardInputSource()
keyboard_name = TISGetInputSourceProperty(keyboard, KTISPropertyLocalizedName)
```

The problem is that the void pointer returned by the function is a direct reference to an object and, therefore, casting it won't work. In this case, because the documentation is clear about the fact that the void pointer is a direct-typed reference, we need to use #to_object on the pointer instead of casting and dereferencing it:

```
framework 'Cocoa'

keyboard = TISCopyCurrentKeyboardInputSource()
keyboard_name = TISGetInputSourceProperty(keyboard, KTISPropertyLocalizedName)
keyboard_name.to_object #=> "U.S."
```

Compilation

A book about MacRuby cannot be complete without mentioning compilation. MacRuby offers two types of compilation: JIT and AOT compilation.

Just In Time compilation (JIT)
> This is the default mode. At runtime, prior to being executed, the source code is optimized and compiled into machine code that can run natively on the machine. Even though this process includes a slight delay at startup time, compiled code usually runs faster than the interpreted code, because MacRuby doesn't have to reevaluate each line of source code each time it is met. This process is totally transparent, since the compilation is done on the fly when a user launches a MacRuby application.

Ahead Of Time compilation (AOT)
> Before execution, source code can be compiled directly into machine code (see the Wikipedia entry for Mach-O file at *http://en.wikipedia.org/wiki/Mach-O*). AOT compilation has two major advantages: it improves startup time and it obfuscates the application source code.

Here is the simplest AOT example—save the following line of code in a file called *hello_world.rb*:

```
p ARGV.join(' ').upcase
```

Or, using the command line, create the file and its content:

```
$ echo "p ARGV.join(' ').upcase" > hello_world.rb
```

The code takes all the passed arguments, joins them together separated by a space, and makes the result string uppercase.

Our "program" source code is now ready, so let's compile it using the MacRuby compiler command line tool, called *macrubyc*:

```
$ macrubyc hello_world.rb -o macruby_says
```

The -o option defines the output file. We can now execute our newly compiled program:

```
$ ./macruby_says hello world
# => "HELLO WORLD"
```

Looking at the *macrubyc* help, we can see that many other options are available:

```
$ macrubyc --help
Usage: macrubyc [options] file...
    -c                            Compile and assemble, but do not link
    -o <file>                     Place the output into <file>
        --static                  Create a standalone static executable
        --framework <name>        Link standalone static executable with given
                                  framework
        --sdk <path>              Use SDK when compiling standalone static
                                  executable
        --dylib                   Create a dynamic library
        --compatibility_version <VERSION>
                                  Compatibility Version for linking
        --current_version <VERSION>  Current Version for linking
        --install_name <NAME>     Install Name for linking
    -C                            Compile, assemble, and link a loadable object
                                  file
    -a, --arch <ARCH>             Compile for specified CPU architecture
    -v, --version                 Display the version
    -V, --verbose                 Print every command line executed
    -h, --help                    Display this information
```

If you look at the contents of a compiled MacRuby application package, you might notice some *.rbo* files. These files are compiled and loadable object files generated using the equivalent of the following command:

```
$ macrubyc -C -o file.rbo file.rb
```

MacRuby can then load the file directly without having to reevaluate it.

Compilation Within Xcode

In most cases, you will use Xcode to develop your application, and the Xcode templates come with a target that does all the work for you. It turns out that there isn't much to do to compile an app. If you open an existing MacRuby project in Xcode and look at the project's target information, you will see that the only thing the target does is to call *macruby_deploy* as such:

```
$ /usr/local/bin/macruby_deploy --compile --embed
```

Because no arguments are passed to define the application-bundle path, macruby_deploy relies on two environment variables set by Xcode to define the location of the bundle: TARGET_BUILD_DIR and PROJECT_NAME.

When called with the `--compile` option, `macruby_deploy` compiles all the Ruby files available in the resources folder. Xcode copies the source files to this folder automatically for you when you build your project, before calling the external script. These files are compiled as *.rbo* files that are loaded by the *rb_main.rb* file.

When the `--embed` option is set, the MacRuby framework is copied to the application bundle, freeing the application from the need to have MacRuby installed on the user's system. As part of this process, the linkage is also modified so the compiled code doesn't break when it's run on a different machine.

Another useful option that you might need to use when compiling an application from Xcode using `macruby_deploy` is `--no-stdlib`. It allows you to make your application smaller by not embedding Ruby's standard library when embedding MacRuby. If you don't rely on any libraries from the standard library, it's recommended that you use this option. If, however, you do rely on a library from the Ruby standard library, you can tell `macruby_deploy` to embed only specific libraries using the `--stdlib` option. It takes the names of one or more libraries. You can also embed Ruby gems libraries, as explained in Chapter 13.

Finally, if you generate some BridgeSupport files or want to force the use of your versions, you can use the `--bs` option to embed them.

The way compilation currently works in Xcode is that you need to run the second target after building your project. In other words, you will usually develop without compiling. When you are ready, change the target to use the provided Deployment scheme, which calls *macruby_deploy*, which itself might call the MacRuby compiler if needed. You can see the available *macruby_deploy* flags by calling its help in the command line, as follows:

```
$ macruby_deploy --help
Usage: macruby_deploy [options] application-bundle
        --compile                 Compile the bundle source code
        --embed                   Embed MacRuby inside the bundle
        --no-stdlib               Do not embed the standard library
        --stdlib [LIB]            Embed only LIB from the standard library
        --gem [GEM]               Embed GEM and its dependencies
        --bs                      Embed the system BridgeSupport files
        --verbose                 Log all commands to standard out
    -v, --version                 Display the version
```

After you run the Deployment scheme, you can start your application manually or go back to your original scheme and build your app again. If the deployment doesn't work as expected, you can look in Xcode's Log navigator to see exactly what happened. You can also set the `--verbose` flag in the target information to see even more information about what *macruby_deploy* does. You can also run *macruby_deploy* manually in the command line, passing it the path to the application bundle file.

Finally, if things don't seem to work properly and you can't figure out what is going on, don't hesitate to clean (Shift + Command + K) the project and build it again.

## PART II

MacRuby in Practice

This part covers concrete examples of applications you might want to develop in MacRuby. While the first part focuses on the theory, this part focuses on actual implementations of given features.

## CHAPTER 9

Address Book Example

The first full example in this book shows how to write an application around Twitter and the Address Book. The goal here is to import our Twitter contacts into our address book and learn new tricks as we go along.

Let's begin by creating a MacRuby application using Xcode. For that, start Xcode and choose the MacRuby template. In the template settings, set the Product Name to TwitterContactImporter and use "clear" or "deselect" or "disable" the Document-Based and Core Data options.

User Interface

I personally find it easier to start by working on the UI, and then adding the required code. Click on the *.xib* file to edit the interface, then select the Window object, as shown in Figure 9-1.

We are going to add a button that will automatically import our Twitter contacts. Once the contacts are imported, we will display the list of our contacts and let the user search for a specific contact.

To start, we need to use an image to put on our button. Head to the Twitter logos and icons site (*http://twitter.com/about/resources/logos*) and download the logo of your choice. Save the image as *twitter_logo.png* somewhere on your hard drive. Once the image is saved, drag and drop it in Xcode into the *Resources* folder. An option screen like the one shown in Figure 9-2 will open.

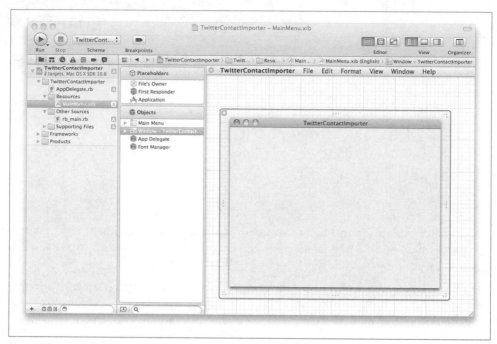

Figure 9-1. Initial UI

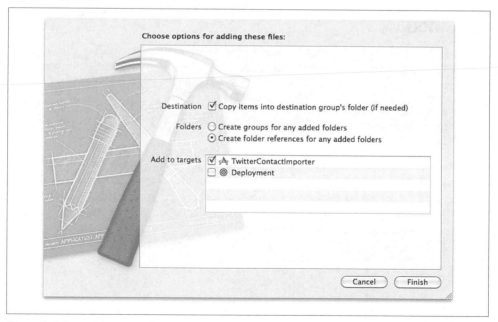

Figure 9-2. Import image option screen

Make sure to select the destination box.

Now, drag a Square Button from the Object Library to the window view, as shown in Figure 9-3.

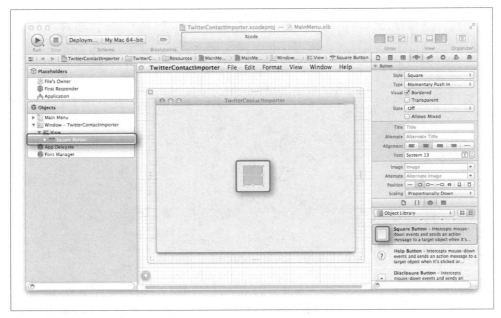

Figure 9-3. Addition of a square button

Let's add our Twitter logo to our button. To do that, select the button and select the Attributes inspector. Open the drop-down menu for the Image attribute and choose `twitter_logo`. Now resize the button to make it bigger. Resizing the button is easy: just use the handles on the sides of the button. Once you are satisfied, make sure the TwitterContactImporter scheme is selected and click Run to compile your application and preview your UI (Figure 9-4). We can also use the document simulator (in the Editor menu), but since the MacRuby source code doesn't have to be compiled, I think it's just as easy and more reliable to run the real app.

If you try to close the window, you will notice that the application is still in the dock. Let's add a line of code to exit the application once the main window is closed. Open *AppDelegate.rb* and add the following code at the bottom of the `AppDelegate` class (i.e., before the last "end"):

```
def windowWillClose(sender); exit; end
```

Before testing this code, we need to do one more thing. We need to tell our window to use our `AppDelegate` so our callback will work as expected. Edit the *.xib* file, right-click

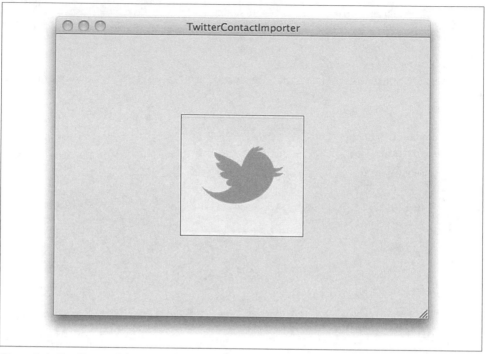

Figure 9-4. Final view of the running application

on the Window instance, and drag the window delegate outlet to the App Delegate object. At this point, the window will delegate everything to our `AppDelegate` instance, which is what we want, since that's where we defined the `windowWillClose` delegate method. Depending on the application you write, you might want to write a window-specific delegate.

Run the application one more time, and notice that this time, when closing the window, the application exits.

Address Book

To use the AddressBook framework, we need first to load it. Edit *rb_main.rb* and on the line loading the Cocoa framework, add the following code:

```
framework 'AddressBook'
```

Earlier, in "Method Missing" on page 153, we examined how to wrap the `Address Book` Cocoa API to make it easier to work with. I wrote a bunch of basic wrappers for the `AddressBook` API. Let's add them to our project.

Right-click the *TwitterContactImporter* folder in the Project navigator and choose New Group. Name the folder Wrappers. Download the wrapper files for this chapter from the book repository and drag them in the *Wrappers* folder (the wrapper files are named *ab*_* and you will also see a file adding some helper methods to Ruby). When the option screen displays, choose to copy the items into the destination group. The files reopen some `AddressBook` classes and add some convenient methods. The files will be automatically loaded by the *rb_main.rb* file.

Next, we need to load the user's address book and make sure the user marked a record as her own. Let's start by creating an accessor for the user's address book. We want to do that when the application finishes launching. Edit *AppDelegte.rb*, add a new attribute reader called `address_reader`, and set its value inside the *applicationDidFinishLaunching* method as follows:

```
class AppDelegate
  attr_accessor :window
  attr_reader :address_book

  def applicationDidFinishLaunching(a_notification)
    @address_book = ABAddressBook.sharedAddressBook
  end

  def windowWillClose(sender); exit; end
end
```

Let's also add a method to alert the user if something goes wrong, such as, for instance, if she didn't set a contact as her own:

```
def alert(title='Alert', message='Something went wrong: ')
  NSAlert.alertWithMessageText(title,
                               defaultButton: 'OK',
                               alternateButton: nil,
                               otherButton: nil,
                               informativeTextWithFormat: message).runModal
end
```

And now let's verify that the user marked an account as hers. If not, let's display a warning:

```
def check_me
  unless address_book.me
    alert "Address Book Problem",
    "You need to open the Address Book and mark a contact as yours. Choose a contact,
    click on Card, and select 'Make this my card'."
  end
end
```

And call our newly created method from inside `applicationDidFinishLaunching`:

```
def applicationDidFinishLaunching(a_notification)
  @address_book = ABAddressBook.sharedAddressBook
  check_me
end
```

This is a good first step, but we also need to check that we set our Twitter nickname in the address book. Without this nickname representing the user's Twitter account, we can't find her contacts. Notice that only public Twitter accounts are supported.

Add the following code at the bottom of the check_me method:

```
if address_book.me.nickname.nil? || address_book.me.nickname == ''
  alert "Address Book Problem",
  "You need to set your Twitter account as your nickname in your contact card."
end
```

Great, so now we have now created a warning that will inform the user if her contact card doesn't contain the information we need. But we also need to create a new contact group to store all the Twitter contacts and keep them somewhat isolated:

```
def create_twitter_group
  twitter_group = address_book.groups.find{|g| g.name == 'Twitter'}
  if twitter_group
    twitter_group
  else
    group = ABGroup.alloc.init
    group.name = 'Twitter'
    puts "adding Twitter group"
    address_book << group
    address_book.save
    twitter_group
  end
end
```

We are going to use this method in a minute, when we call the web API.

Web API Call

Now that the Twitter information is ready, we can write the code that will be called to fetch the Twitter contacts when the user clicks our Twitter button.

In Cocoa terms, such a method is called an *action*. We will connect our button's performClick event to a new method, passing as its argument the instance that calls the method. Here is the action code:

```
def import_twitter_contacts(sender)
  me = address_book.me
  twitter_group = create_twitter_group
  puts "Importing from Twitter"

  Thread.new{
    fetch_paginated_friends(me.nickname) do |friends|
      puts "Importing a batch of friends"
      add_twitter_friends(friends, twitter_group)
    end
    address_book.save
    puts "Import done"
  }

end
```

This code calls a method that we haven't implemented yet, named fetch_paginated_friends. And for each batch of retrieved friends, we add them to the newly created group, using a new method called `add_twitter_friends`. Finally, when all the friends have been imported, the address book is saved.

The reason the code is wrapped in a new thread is so we don't block the main loop. Because our application is very simple, using the main thread wouldn't have been a big deal. Indeed, a user can't do anything else in the application while we're loading contacts, so making him wait until the import is done wouldn't be too bad. However, this is a bad practice and, as you can see, running the code in a separate thread is really straightforward.

Let's connect our button to this action. To do that, select the *MainMenu.xib* file, right-click on the App Delegate icon, and drag the circle attached to import_twitter_contacts (in the Received Action submenu) to the big button we added.

Now let's implement the paginated fetching, using the Twitter API (*http://dev.twitter.com/doc*):

```
def fetch_paginated_friends(account, &block)
  cursor = '-1'
  until cursor == 0
    url_string =
      "http://twitter.com/statuses/friends/#{account}.json?cursor=#{cursor}"
    url = NSURL.alloc.initWithString(url_string)
    json_friends   = NSMutableString.alloc.initWithContentsOfURL(url,
                                             encoding:NSUTF8StringEncoding,
                                             error:nil)

    friend_results = JSON.parse(json_friends)
    block.call(friend_results['users'])
    cursor = friend_results['next_cursor']
  end
end
```

The code isn't complicated, but it mixes some Cocoa API calls with some advanced Ruby idioms. The first thing you might notice is that the second method argument starts with an ampersand and looks funny. It's Ruby's way of saying that this method expects to be called with a block. The method can't be called without passing a block.

The Twitter API uses the principle of a *cursor* to paginate through the results. The first page starts at cursor −1 and each result set contains information about the previous or next cursor. When there aren't any pages to iterate through, the cursor is set to 0. Because of this, we can write our code so it will keep calling the Twitter API until a response defines the next cursor as 0. The data coming back from the API is a string in the JSON format. To parse this data, we first need to require the JSON library at the top of the file, as follows:

```
require 'json'
```

That's the library used to parse the body of the API response. We then extract a subset of this data and send it to our block, like this:

```
block.call(friend_results['users'])
```

This calls the passed block and passes it our data subset as a parameter. Look at how we called this method and used the block. See that the block's parameter is called friends? Our implementation executes the passed block and replaces "friends" with the data subset so that it can be manipulated from within the block:

```
fetch_paginated_friends(me.nickname) do |friends|
  # do something with a subset of the friends
end
```

For our code to work, we also need to implement the add_twitter_friends method that is called from within the block:

```
def add_twitter_friends(friends, group)
  friends.each do |friend|
    # avoid duplicates
    if friend['screen_name']
      query = ABPerson.searchElementForProperty(KABNicknameProperty,
                  label:nil, key:nil, value:friend['screen_name'],
                  comparison:KABEqual)
      results = address_book.recordsMatchingSearchElement(query)
      contact = results.first || ABPerson.alloc.initWithAddressBook(address_book)
    else
      contact = ABPerson.alloc.initWithAddressBook(address_book)
    end

    first_name, last_name = friend['name'].split(' ')
    contact.firstName = first_name if first_name
    contact.lastName  = last_name if last_name
    contact.nickname  = friend['screen_name']
    urls = {'Twitter' => "http://twitter.com/#{friend['screen_name']}"}
    urls[KABHomePageLabel] = friend['url'] unless friend['url'].blank?
    contact.URLs  = urls.to_ab_multivalue

    contact.imageData = NSData.dataWithContentsOfURL(friend['profile_image_url'].\
                                                     to_nsurl)

    notes = []
    notes << friend['description'] unless friend['description'].blank?
    notes << "Location: #{friend['location']}" unless friend['location'].blank?
    contact.note = notes.join("\n")

    group << contact
  end

end
```

Even though this method is a bit long, what it does is very simple. For each friend in the passed array, it checks whether a matching record already exists in the address book. If so, the method updates the record based on the information returned by Twitter, or creates a new record. We even download the profile image and assign it as the contact's image. Once the method is done parsing the data, the updated/created contact is added to the group. Voilà!

Cleaning Up: Better Management of Widgets

The application we've thrown together is great, but we have a few issues to fix and features to add. First, a user might click multiple times on the button, and that would run our fetching code in multiple parallel threads. We obviously don't want that. The other thing is that the user isn't notified that the contacts are being fetched. Let's fix that!

The first thing to do is give our code access to our big Twitter button. By now, you should know what we need to do:

1. Add a button attribute accessor in our class so Xcode sees it as an outlet.
2. In the Interface Builder, right-click the App Delegate icon and assign the button outlet to the big Twitter button.

In this section, instead of using the Interface Builder tool provided by Xcode, we are going to set the rest of the UI programmatically. This is mostly meant as an exercise and to show you that it is not that hard after all.

Now that we have access to our button, we want to hide the button after it was clicked and show a progress indicator. To do that, let's create a method and dispatch it from the button action:

```
def make_user_wait
  button.hidden = true
  if @spinner
    @spinner.hidden = false
  else
    x = window.frame.size.width/2 - 32/2
    y = window.frame.size.height/2 - 32/2
    @spinner = NSProgressIndicator.alloc.initWithFrame([x,y,32,32])
    @spinner.style = NSProgressIndicatorSpinningStyle
    window.contentView.addSubview(@spinner)
  end
  @spinner.startAnimation(nil)
end
```

This code is a bit more complicated than it should be, but it shows how to display a view item in relation to another one. The first thing we do is hide the Twitter button Then, if the spinner already exists, we show it, otherwise we create an instance that we locate exactly at the middle of the window. To do that, we calculate the x and y positions by inspecting the window frame size and locating the indicator in the center, based on its size in pixels (32×32). We also need to start the spinning animation.

The only problem is that we tell the users to wait, but then don't show them anything. Thankfully, Cocoa has a widget that lets you integrate a contact browser in your app. Let's add it to our sample and display the contact browser once all the contacts are imported. Our `import_twitter_contacts` method will look like this:

```
def import_twitter_contacts(sender)

  make_user_wait
  me = address_book.me
  twitter_group = create_twitter_group
  puts "Importing from Twitter"

  Thread.new{
    fetch_paginated_friends(me.nickname) do |friends|
      puts "Importing a batch of friends"
      add_twitter_friends(friends, twitter_group)
    end
    address_book.save
    puts "Import done"
    display_contacts
  }

end
```

And `display_contacts` looks like this:

```
def display_contacts
  @spinner.stopAnimation(nil)
  @spinner.hidden = true
  frame = [0,0, window.frame.size.width, window.frame.size.height - 120]
  @picker = ABPeoplePickerView.alloc.initWithFrame(frame)
  window.contentView.addSubview(@picker)
end
```

Again, the code is straightforward. We stop the spinner and hide it. We then create an instance of `ABPeoplePickerView` that will be slightly shorter than the window's height. Once the instance is created, we add it to our window's content view.

The Extra Mile: Displaying More Information Through Notifications

What we have done already is really cool, but it would be even nicer to display some of the contact's details while browsing them. We can do this by adding more UI elements and by observing the interaction with the `ABPeoplePickerView`.

This time, instead of creating UI elements and placing them programmatically on the window, let's set our elements but hide them until we need them. Before we do that, let's add some outlets for all of the UI elements and, while we are at it, add an attribute reader for the picker:

```
class AppDelegate
  attr_accessor :window, :button
  attr_reader :address_book, :picker
  attr_accessor :contact_name, :contact_image, :contact_twitter

  #...
end
```

Next, add an `ImageWell` instance of 100x100 on the top left of your UI. Edit the Image view's settings and change the drop-down to make the view scale proportionally up or down. Then, to the right of the image, add two labels. Before you hide them all, right-click the app delegate icon and connect your three outlets to your new UI items. Now, go to each of them and set their drawing attributes to hidden.

Now we just need to write the code displaying the hidden UI items, setting up the notification center and its callback method:

```
def display_contacts
  @spinner.stopAnimation(nil)
  @spinner.hidden = true
  frame = [0,0, window.frame.size.width, window.frame.size.height - 120]
  @picker = ABPeoplePickerView.alloc.initWithFrame(frame)
  center = NSNotificationCenter.defaultCenter
  center.addObserver(self,
                     selector: "record_changed:",
                     name: ABPeoplePickerNameSelectionDidChangeNotification,
                     object:picker)
  picker.allowsMultipleSelection = false
  picker.addProperty KABNicknameProperty
  contact_image.hidden = false
  contact_name.hidden = false
  contact_twitter.hidden = false
  window.contentView.addSubview(picker)
end
```

In "Notification Centers" on page 63, we covered the notification center and observers. The principle is simple: when the user changes the selected contact, the callback selector is called. The following code implements the callback method, which simply finds the selected record and sets the UI elements with the record's data:

```
def record_changed(notification)
  selected = picker.selectedRecords || []
  if selected.empty?
    contact_image.image = nil
    contact_name.stringValue = ""
    contact_twitter.stringValue = ""
  else
    person = selected.first
    contact_image.image = NSImage.alloc.initWithData(person.imageData)
    contact_name.stringValue = "#{person.firstName} #{person.lastName}"
    contact_twitter.stringValue  = person.nickname || ''
  end
end
```

Our app is now finished. After running the app and playing a bit with it, you can open your *AddressBook.app* and see all your Twitter contacts being imported and their details becoming available, as shown in Figure 9-5.

Figure 9-5. My Twitter contacts imported and previewed

## CHAPTER 10

Geolocation

The example in this chapter shows how to write an application that uses the user's geographical location and a location web service. To do that, we are going to use the `CoreLocation` framework, the *gowalla.com* web API (offering location information based on coordinates), and a `TableView` instance.

As before, we start by creating a MacRuby application using Xcode. Start Xcode and choose the MacRuby template. In the template settings, set the Product Name to "AroundMe" and disable the Document-Based and Core Data options.

User Interface

In this example, the UI will be very simple. We are going to work with just an `NSTable View` instance and a bunch of columns (`NSTableColumn`).

Edit your *.xib* file and resize the main window to be 640 pixels by 440 pixels (use the Size Inspector in the Utilities panel). Now drag and drop a Table View from the Object Library inside the Window's view. Using the grid guides, scale the table to use most of the window's real estate.

At this point, make sure the AroundMe scheme is selected and click Run. The app should look like Figure 10-1.

We are going to use the Gowalla API (*http://gowalla.com/api/docs*) to find the locations (called *spots* in Gowalla's jargon) around our users. You can see the type of information the API provides us by going to the following page: *http://gowalla.com/api/explorer#/ spots?lat=30.2697&lng=-97.7494&radius=50*.

We can't easily display all the spot's information. Instead, we are going to filter the data and display only the following:

- The spot's category
- The spot's name
- The spot's description

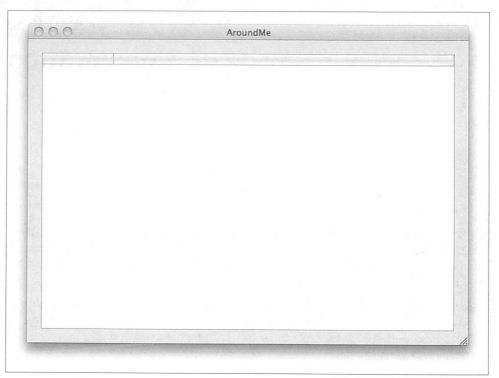

Figure 10-1. Blank Table View

- The spot's distance
- The number of items in the spot
- The number of users who visited this spot
- The number of checkins in the spot

Let's add some columns to our table. The easiest way to do that is to copy/paste an existing table column. The end result should look like Figure 10-2.

Now, let's name each column's header by setting the header cell title via the Attributes Inspector (Figure 10-3).

Our first column will display an image, so we need to change the type of cell it uses. Drag and drop an Image Cell inside the first column so the Text Field cell gets replaced by its Image counterpart (Figure 10-4).

Finally, one by one, edit the table columns and use the Attributes Inspector to make sure the columns are not editable.

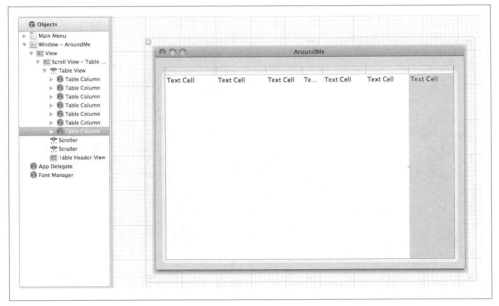

Figure 10-2. Seven table columns added

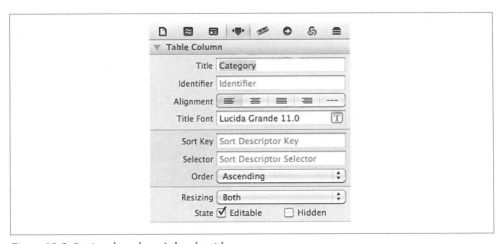

Figure 10-3. Setting the column's header title

 You can select all the columns at once and set the flag the way you want it.

That's enough for the UI for now. Let's move on to writing some code.

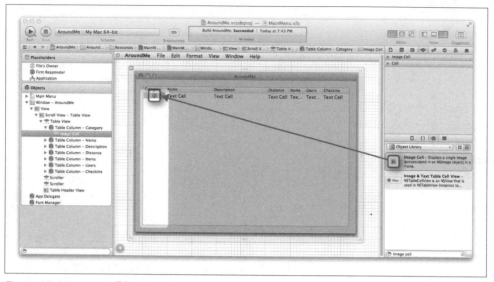

Figure 10-4. Image Cell being used in the first column

Table View

Before we get to call the web API and fetch the information, we need to wire the table view. We are going to call our table **spot_table** and create an outlet for it in our *App-Delegate.rb* file:

```
class AppDelegate
  attr_accessor :window
  attr_accessor :spot_table

  ...
end
```

Going back to the UI editor, right-click the App Delegate object, choose the **spot_table** outlet, and connect it to the table view.

Connect the outlet to the table view, not the scroll view. The table view is inside the scroll view.

We can now initialize the table view delegation as follows:

```
def applicationDidFinishLaunching(a_notification)
  spot_table.dataSource = self
  spot_table.doubleAction = "preview:"
end
```

Setting the `TableView` instance's dataSource to `self` means that we are expected to implement the table's methods in our `AppDelegate` class (which is what `self` refers to in this context). We are also setting the `doubleAction` selector, representing the action to dispatch when a row is double-clicked. Of course, that means that we will need to implement this action in a minute.

For the table to work properly, we need to implement a few methods. But before we get there, we need to define an object that will hold the references to spots. Our table will use this object to fetch and sort its content. Let's call this object `@spots`, make an attribute accessor for it, and initialize it as an empty array when the application finishes loading. We are going to use this object as the table data source. For more information about how to use a table data source, please read the Apple developer page, About Table Views in Mac OS X Applications (*http://developer.apple.com/library/mac/#docu mentation/Cocoa/Conceptual/TableView/Introduction/Introduction.html*).

This is how our `AppDelegate` class should look:

```
class AppDelegate
  attr_accessor :window
  attr_accessor :spots, :spot_table

  def applicationDidFinishLaunching(a_notification)
    @spots = []
    spot_table.dataSource = self
    spot_table.doubleAction = "preview:"
  end

  def windowWillClose(sender); exit; end

end
```

 I skipped the `windowWillClose` delegate explanation here because I covered it many times previously. Remember that you need to set the window's delegate to the `AppDelegate` class.

Now that we defined our data source object, we can define some table delegate methods based on this reference object. One of these methods indicates to the table view the number of records in the source:

```
def numberOfRowsInTableView(view)
  spots.size
end
```

We also need to implement some sort of overloaded method. In Objective-C, a single method name can be defined with different method signatures. MacRuby supports the same approach when a hash is used in the method signature. We are going to implement the following methods:

```
def tableView(view, objectValueForTableColumn:column, row:index)
end

def tableView(view, sortDescriptorsDidChange:descriptors)
end
```

These are two alternative signatures defined by the `TableView` API. The first method retrieves the value for a given column, whereas the second defines sorting in the table. In both, the second argument is a hash object (Ruby 1.9 style), but the keys are different between the two method signatures.

When the first method is dispatched, it is passed the column object and row index to retrieve the data to display. Now we have two issues: we don't have any data to look at yet, and we don't have a way to look up a record's value with a column instance as a key. To make things easier, we are going to edit our columns and set their editors with the matching JSON key we are getting from the web API call. Once we implement the web API fetching, we will wrap each spot in an object that will respond to the key names. We can also directly look up the values in the JSON object, but that won't allow us to customize and massage the data easily, since the JSON data structure is somewhat limited.

In the UI editor, select each column and set the identifier as follows:

- Category → image
- Name → name
- Description → description
- Distance → radius_meters
- Items → items_count
- Users → users
- Checkins → checkins

The implementation of the first method is as follows:

```
def tableView(view, objectValueForTableColumn:column, row:index)
  spot = spots[index]
  id = column.identifier
  if id == 'image'
    # NSImageCell instance, we need to feed it an NSImage
    @cell_images ||= {}
    @cell_images[spot.image] ||= NSImage.alloc.initWithData(
      NSURL.URLWithString(spot.image).resourceDataUsingCache(true)
    )
  else
    spot.send(id.to_sym)
  end
end
```

The first thing we are doing in this method is fetching the spot based on its index in the data source. We then extract the column identifier and check whether it matches the *image* string. If it does, we allocate a new `NSImage` instance based on the image URL that was fetched from the web API. To improve performance, we are *memoizing* all the NSImage instances we create and making sure to use the built-in cache. Finally, for all other columns, we are dispatching the identifier's method using Ruby's #send method, which takes, as its argument, the method's name as a symbol (#to_sym converts a string into a symbol).

We'll keep the second method very simple for now. Instead of doing anything here, we will just reload the data for the moment:

```
def tableView(view, sortDescriptorsDidChange:descriptors)
  spot_table.reloadData
end
```

Core Location

Before we can call Gowalla's API, we still need to get the user's location. For that, we are going to use CoreLocation, a framework available in OS X that allows the user to share his geographical location with a given program.

The CLLocationManager class, available from CoreLocation (see *http://developer.apple .com/library/mac/#documentation/CoreLocation/Reference/CoreLocation_Framework/ _index.html*) framework, does all the work, but it's a bit clumsy. So let's write a thin wrapper to keep our delegate class simpler. Add a new Ruby file called location_man ager.rb and paste the following code in the file:

```
framework 'CoreLocation'
# CLLocationManager wrapper
class LocationManager

  def initialize(&block)
    @loc         = CLLocationManager.alloc.init
    @loc.delegate = self
    @callback    = block
  end

  def start
    @loc.startUpdatingLocation
  end

  def stop
    @loc.stopUpdatingLocation
  end

  # Dispatch the CLLocationManager callback to the Ruby callback
  def locationManager(manager, didUpdateToLocation: new_location,
                               fromLocation: old_location)
    @callback.call(new_location, self)
  end

end
```

This wrapper doesn't do much, but it will make our code cleaner. We basically define a new class called LocationManager, which expects a block at initiation. The block is kept in memory and is called when new location information is retrieved. I also added two simple instance methods, #start and #stop, which delegate to the underlying CLLocationManager instance. There is documentation for CoreLocation (*http://developer .apple.com/library/ios/#documentation/CoreLocation/Reference/CLLocationManager _Class/CLLocationManager/CLLocationManager.html*) at the Apple developer site.

This nice wrapper allows us to print a location like this:

```
location_manager = LocationManager.new do |new_location, manager|
  puts "location: #{new_location.description}"
  manager.stop
end
location_manager.start
```

As a matter of fact, you can put the wrapper and the previous code in a file and get your location that way. You will need to add the following line at the bottom of the file to keep the run loop running:

```
NSRunLoop.currentRunLoop.runUntilDate(NSDate.distantFuture)
```

Execute the file using MacRuby, and you should be presented with a dialog box like the one shown in Figure 10-5.

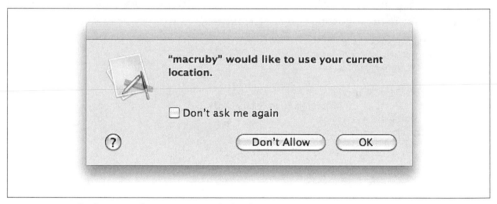

Figure 10-5. The location-sharing security dialog box

And something like this should be printed out on your terminal:

```
location: <+32.67000000, 117.24000000> +/- 181.00m
            (speed -1.00 mps / course -1.00) @ 2011-05-15 22:46:24 -0700
```

Back to our app. Let's use our wrapper in our applicationDidFinishLaunching callback method:

```
def applicationDidFinishLaunching(notification)
  @spots = []
  location_manager = LocationManager.new do |new_location, manager|
    puts "location: #{new_location.description}"
```

```
      gowalla = gowalla_req(new_location)
      @spots  = gowalla['spots'].map{|spot| GowallaSpot.new(spot)}
      @spots.sort!{|a,b| a.radius_meters <=> b.radius_meters}
      spot_table.reloadData
      manager.stop
    end

    spot_table.dataSource = self
    spot_table.doubleAction = "preview:"
    location_manager.start
  end
```

Within the block, we are making a Gowalla call, iterating through the spots, and storing them in an array of `GowallaSpot` instances. The spots are then sorted based on their distances. The table view reloads its data and the location manager is stopped.

The location manager obviously cannot be started from within the callback block, so we need to start it once everything is set up. That's what we do before closing the method definition.

Web API

Right now, this code won't work. We still need to implement the `GowallaSpot` class and the `#gowalla_req` method. I personally like to write high-level code before I implement the underlying methods; I feel it helps me design my APIs better.

The `GowallaSpot` class is very straightforward. Create a new file with the following code:

```
class GowallaSpot

  attr_reader :name
  attr_reader :url
  attr_reader :description
  attr_reader :highlights_url
  attr_reader :lat, :lgn
  attr_reader :image
  attr_reader :items_count
  attr_reader :radius_meters
  attr_reader :users, :checkins

  def initialize(spot_hash)
    @name = spot_hash['name']
    @url = NSURL.URLWithString(
              "http://gowalla.com#{spot_hash['url']}")
    @description = spot_hash['description']
    @highlights_url = 'http://gowalla.com'  \
      + spot_hash['highlights_url']
    @lat = spot_hash['lat']
    @lgn = spot_hash['lgn']
    @image = spot_hash['_image_url_50']
    @items_count = spot_hash['items_count']
    @radius_meters = spot_hash['radius_meters']
    @users = spot_hash['users_count']
```

```
      @checkins = spot_hash['checkins_count']
    end

  end
```

The #gowalla_req method is defined inside the AppDelegate class like this:

```
def gowalla_req(location)
  http = Net::HTTP.start('api.gowalla.com')
  req = Net::HTTP::Get.new("/spots?lat=#{location.coordinate.latitude}&" + \
                           "lng=#{location.coordinate.longitude}&radius=500")
  req.add_field("Accept", "application/json")
  req.add_field("X-Gowalla-API-Key", GOWALLA_API_KEY)
  response = http.request(req)
  JSON.parse(response.body)
end
```

This method uses Ruby's net/http library (*http://www.ruby-doc.org/ruby-1.9/classes/ Net/HTTP.html*) to make a call to the Gowalla web API and the built-in JSON library (*http://www.ruby-doc.org/ruby-1.9/classes/JSON.html*). To use these libraries, we need to require them at the top of our file using require "net/http" and require "json". You need to get your own API key from Gowalla (*http://gowalla.com/api/keys*) and store it in the GOWALLA_API_KEY constant.

If you run the app, everything should load properly and you will see the various spots around you. It's nice, but we are missing one last thing: the preview action. Remember that earlier we set a selector to trigger when a user double-clicks a row. Let's implement this preview action:

```
def preview(sender)
  if spot_table.selectedRow >= 0
    url = spots[spot_table.selectedRow].url
    NSWorkspace.sharedWorkspace.openURL(url)
  end
end
```

NSWorkspace.sharedWorkspace.openURL (see *http://developer.apple.com/library/mac/ #documentation/Cocoa/Reference/ApplicationKit/Classes/NSWorkspace_Class/Refer ence/Reference.html*) opens a given URL in the user's default browser. We made sure that when this method is called, the table has a valid selected row and we retrieve the URL by accessing the spots data source using the row index.

If you run the application now, you should be able to view all the Gowalla spots around you and visit their web pages by double-clicking a row (Figure 10-6).

Category	Name	Description	Distance	Items	Users	Checkins
	Jack In The Box		50	2	10	42
	Home		50	0	3	9
	Mobil Gas Station		50	2	11	42
	Round Table Pizza		75	1	5	15
	Yenchim Garden	Chinese Restaurant	75	1	12	45
	Subway		75	1	6	25
	P.Q. Donuts	It's a nice surprise wh...	75	1	2	4
	Vons		75	1	14	61
	O'Reilly's		75	1	4	25
	Betchay's Pancit L...	Filipino food FTW! try...	75	1	5	14
	Cotijas Mexican Grill		75	1	15	42
	Rpq		75	1	8	27
	Golden Bagel Cafe		75	1	11	24
	Wonderful Sushi	Japanese Restaurant	75	1	6	26
	Cafe 56		75	1	14	25
	Teo's Barber Shop		75	1	4	16
	Bertrand's Music		75	1	7	27
	Carl's Jr.		75	2	12	28
	Bad Ass Coffee		75	1	20	49
	Sushihana	50% off all the time.	75	1	15	38

Figure 10-6. The end result

## CHAPTER 11

MacRuby in Objective-C Projects

MacRuby is great, but you might already have a Cocoa application written in Objective-C. Rewriting all of it in MacRuby would probably be fun, but maybe not really wise. You might also want to experiment with MacRuby without fully committing to it yet. Another reason to mix the two languages is if you want to better test your Objective-C code, but are not pleased by the existing Objective-C tools. Whatever reason you have, MacRuby is really easy to use within your existing app.

API

MacRuby is a framework, so to use it in your Objective-C project, you just need to add it to your project and import the headers:

```
#import <MacRuby/MacRuby.h>
```

Once you have added the framework and imported the headers, you can call out to files or snippets of MacRuby from Objective-C. Let's take a minute to look at the API provided by the MacRuby framework:

```
#import <Foundation/Foundation.h>

@interface MacRuby : NSObject

/* Get a singleton reference to the MacRuby runtime, initializing it before if
 * needed. The same instance is re-used after.
 */
+ (MacRuby *)sharedRuntime;

/* Evaluate a Ruby expression in the given file and return a reference to the
 * result.
 */
- (id)evaluateFileAtPath:(NSString *)path;

/* Evaluate a Ruby expression in the given URL and return a reference to the
 * result. Currently only file:// URLs are supported.
 */
- (id)evaluateFileAtURL:(NSURL *)URL;
```

```
/* Evaluate a Ruby expression in the given string and return a reference to the
 * result.
 */
- (id)evaluateString:(NSString *)expression;

/* Load the BridgeSupport file (<<bridgesupport-intro>>) at the given path.
 */
- (void)loadBridgeSupportFileAtPath:(NSString *)path;

/* Load the BridgeSupport file at the given URL.
 */
- (void)loadBridgeSupportFileAtURL:(NSURL *)URL;

@end

@interface NSObject (MacRubyAdditions)

/* Perform the given selector and return a reference to the result. */
- (id)performRubySelector:(SEL)sel;

/* Perform the given selector, passing the given arguments and return a
 * reference to the result. The argv argument should be a C array whose size
 * is the value of the argc argument.
 */
- (id)performRubySelector:(SEL)sel withArguments:(id *)argv count:(int)argc;

/* Perform the given selector, passing the given arguments and return a
 * reference to the result. The arguments should be a NULL-terminated list.
 */
- (id)performRubySelector:(SEL)sel withArguments:(id)firstArgument, ...;

@end
```

Usage

The MacRuby module you imported is the key channel for turning MacRuby code into
something the Objective-C code can use. In the following code, the module's
`evaluateString` method transforms MacRuby code into a generic object that the
Objective-C code refers to:

```
#import <MacRuby/MacRuby.h>

int main(void) {
  NSString *source =  @"module Greetings def self.hello; NSLog('Hello World!');\
    end; end; Greetings";
  id greetings = [[MacRuby sharedRuntime] evaluateString:source];
  [greetings performRubySelector:@selector(hello)];

  return 0;
}
```

Save the file as *hello_from_macruby.m* and run the following command:

```
$ gcc hello_from_macruby.m -o hello -framework Foundation -framework MacRuby -fobjc-gc
```

Now execute the output file as follows:

```
$ ./hello
2011-05-23 22:39:19.342 hello[90424:903] Hello World!
```

The code doesn't do much. It defines a string called source, which contains some Ruby code. The Ruby code defines a module called Greetings with a hello method, printing the famous "Hello World!" string. The MacRuby string's final statement returns a reference to the Greetings module.

We then evaluate this string using evaluateString, as mentioned, and assign the value returned (the last value returned by the evaluated MacRuby source) to a variable called greetings of type id. Using the id type in Objective-C is a way of casting variables as a generic object type. In other words, it's a way to use dynamic typing in Objective-C.

Once we assign our MacRuby module to an Objective-C variable, the Objective-C class has access to the methods within the MacRuby module. So we can dispatch the hello method by calling performRubySelector: and passing the method as a selector.

We can simplify this example by doing the following:

```
#import <MacRuby/MacRuby.h>

int main(void) {

    NSString *source = [NSString stringWithFormat:@""
    "module Greetings;"
    "  def self.hello;"
    "    NSLog('Hello World!');"
    "  end;"
    "end;"
    "Greetings.hello"];
    [[MacRuby sharedRuntime] evaluateString:source];

    return 0;
}
```

It's the same Ruby code, but instead of calling the hello method from Objective-C, we call it directly in our Ruby source code.

However, you probably don't want to keep Ruby code as strings in your Objective-C code. The easiest way to deal with Ruby source code is to save it in its own file and require it using another API. So let's rewrite our example to save the Ruby code in its own file called *greetings.rb*:

```
module Greetings
  def self.hello
    NSLog('Hello World!')
  end
end
Greetings.hello
```

Now change the implementation file to just "require" our Ruby file:

```
#import <MacRuby/MacRuby.h>

int main(void) {
  [[MacRuby sharedRuntime] evaluateFileAtPath:@"./greetings.rb"];
  return 0;
}
```

Compile the file as shown earlier, and you will notice that the output is the same.

It's important to understand that the code is evaluated but stays in memory. So the following code will work fine and print two "Hello World!" strings:

```
#import <MacRuby/MacRuby.h>

int main(void) {
  [[MacRuby sharedRuntime] evaluateFileAtPath:@"./greetings.rb"];
  [[MacRuby sharedRuntime] evaluateString:@"Greetings.hello"];
  return 0;
}
```

However, each evaluation uses its own local scope, so if you wish to evaluate a Ruby object in two separate calls, you need to make sure the object is available the second time it's called. Consider the following example:

```
#import <MacRuby/MacRuby.h>

int main(void) {
  [[MacRuby sharedRuntime] evaluateString:@"@msg = 'Hello!'"];
  [[MacRuby sharedRuntime] evaluateString:@"puts @msg"];
  return 0;
}
```

In this case, the first evaluation uses a Ruby instance variable (ivars start with @ in Ruby) to store a string. The second evaluation prints this string. The code as shown works fine. But if we were to remove the @ sign in front of the msg and thus convert the instance variable into a local variable, the second evaluation would fail, because the local variable was defined in a different scope.

Earlier, we looked at how to assign a Ruby object to an Objective-C variable. MacRuby can already access all the Objective-C code, but sometimes you want to pass a specific object to your Ruby code. To do that, pass it as a parameter, as follows:

```
#import <MacRuby/MacRuby.h>

int main(void) {
  NSString *source = @"module Helper; def self.swapcase(str); str.swapcase;
end; end";
  [[MacRuby sharedRuntime] evaluateString:source];
  id helper = [[MacRuby sharedRuntime] evaluateString:@"Helper"];
  NSString *result = [helper performRubySelector:@selector(swapcase:)
                                   withArguments:@"MacRuby", nil];
  NSLog(@"%@\n", result);
  return 0;
}
```

Per the API description, we are passing a NULL-terminated list with our argument being an Objective-C variable.

Here is the compilation and execution:

```
$ gcc example.m -o example -framework Foundation -framework MacRuby -fobjc-gc
$ ./example
2011-05-23 23:03:12.142 example[92128:903] mACrUBY
```

Example in an Xcode Project

Until now, we have been using a simple implementation file to explore how to use Ruby code from an Objective-C file. Let's build a full Cocoa project in Objective-C and use MacRuby within the app.

Open Xcode and create a new project using the Cocoa Application template. Call this project EmbeddedMacRuby and don't enable any of the options.

Once the project is created, look at the project's target summary. We need to link the MacRuby framework. Click on the + button, as shown in Figure 11-1.

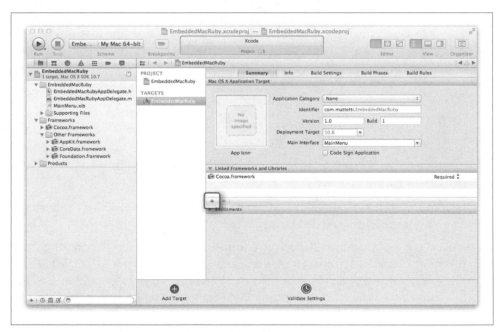

Figure 11-1. Linking the MacRuby framework

Choose the MacRuby framework from the menu and click the Add button. At that point, the framework should appear in the project navigator and you might want to drag it to the framework's subfolder.

While you are editing the settings, you also need to make sure your project uses the Objective-C garbage collector (GC), because MacRuby requires it. Click the Build Settings tab and scroll down until you find the Objective-C Garbage Collection field. Toggle the value and select Required [-fobjc-gc-only] as shown in Figure 11-2.

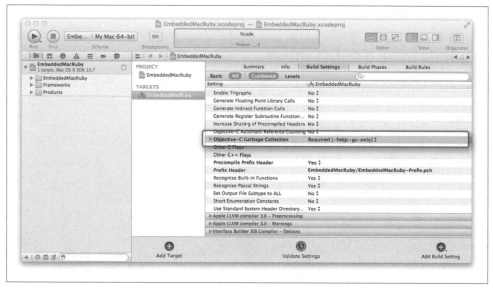

Figure 11-2. Making sure the GC support is marked as required

Now that you have added the framework and set the GC settings, you can import the headers, and your project will build properly.

Edit *EmbeddedMacRubyAppDelegate.m* and add the following import statement:

```
#import <MacRuby/MacRuby.h>
```

To make sure everything is set correctly, run your new project. Everything should build and an empty window should display.

Now that you know that MacRuby is available in our Objective-C project and you know that this project builds correctly, let's build a Ruby interpreter inside your UI. The idea is to write and execute/evaluate Ruby code from within the app as it is running. While this is a demo exercise, I'm sure you can imagine how useful it might be to debug an existing Objective-C app.

User Interface

As usual, we will set the UI first. Start by editing *MainMenu.xib* and expand the Window and View objects. Drag and drop a Horizontal Split View from the Object Library (Utilities Panel), as shown in Figure 11-3.

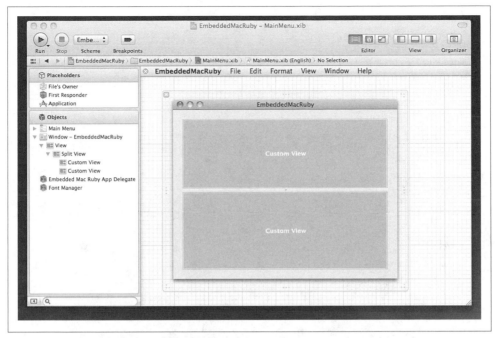

Figure 11-3. Setting up a horizontal split view

We are going to use the upper part of the split view to type in Ruby code and the lower part to show the result. Go back to the Object Library and drag a Text View in the top Custom View into the Split View. Also drag in a label, change the text to read "Ruby Code," and organize the UI to look like Figure 11-4.

Do the same for the lower part, and add a button to trigger evaluation of the code. The end result should look like Figure 11-5.

You will also want to tweak the Split View and the Text views to autoresize (Figure 11-6).

Using the MacRuby Method

Now that the UI looks good, let's write some code. Edit *EmbeddedMacRubyAppDelegate.h* and add two outlets, one for each text view. Also add an action for our button. Your header file should look like this:

```
#import <Cocoa/Cocoa.h>

@interface EmbeddedMacRubyAppDelegate : NSObject <NSApplicationDelegate> {
  IBOutlet NSTextView *rubySourceTextView;
  IBOutlet NSTextView *resultTextView;

@private
  NSWindow *window;
```

```
}

- (IBAction)evaluate:(id)sender;

@property (assign) IBOutlet NSWindow *window;

@end
```

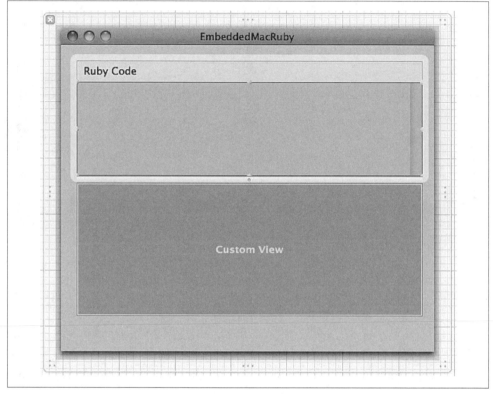

Figure 11-4. Text field to input some Ruby code

Go back to the Interface Builder and right-click Embedded Mac Ruby App Delegate. Drag the rubySourceTextView outlet to the upper scroll view, the resultTextView to the lower scroll view, and the evaluate: action to the push button. Your UI is now wired to your delegate class.

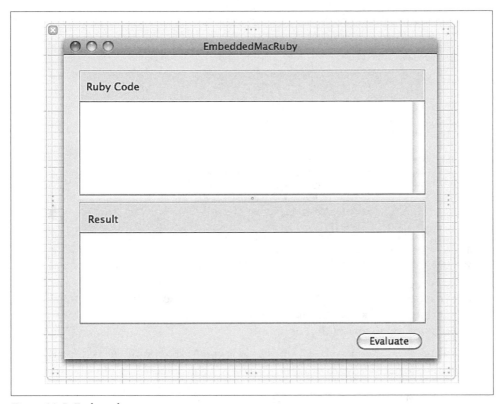

Figure 11-5. End result

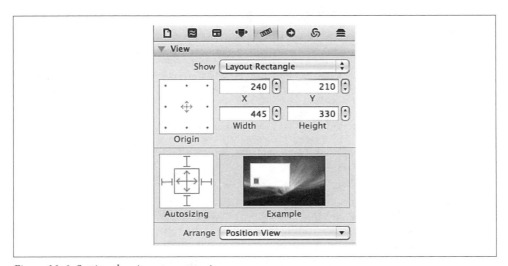

Figure 11-6. Setting the views to autoresize

Edit the *EmbeddedMacRubyAppDelegate.m* implementation file and add an `awakeFrom Nib` method:

```
- (void)awakeFromNib
{
  NSFont *niceFont;

  niceFont = [NSFont fontWithName:@"Monaco" size:12.0];
  [rubySourceTextView setFont:niceFont];
  [resultTextView setFont:niceFont];

  NSString *demoSource = [NSString stringWithFormat: @""
      "@window = NSWindow.alloc.initWithContentRect(\n"
      "          [200,100,200,200],\n"
      "          styleMask:NSTitledWindowMask,\n"
      "          backing:NSBackingStoreBuffered,\n"
      "          defer:false)\n"
      "@window.BackgroundColor = NSColor.blueColor\n"
      "@window.orderFront(NSApp)"];
  [rubySourceTextView setString:demoSource];
}
```

Even if you are not familiar with Objective-C, this code should be understandable. We start by setting the same font for the views of our Ruby source and our result text. Then we insert some demo text in the source view.

This method is called when the UI finishes loading. At that point, everything is set for the user and he needs only to press the button to create a new window.

You can now run the app. It should build fine and the UI will display properly with the sample text in the source text view. But a warning should let you know that the `evaluate` action implementation is missing. Let's add it:

```
- (IBAction)evaluate:(id)sender
{
  @try {
    id object;

    object = [[MacRuby sharedRuntime] evaluateString:[rubySourceTextView string]];
    [resultTextView setString:[object description]];
  }
  @catch (NSException *exception) {
    NSString *string = [NSString stringWithFormat:@"%@: %@\n%@",
                          [exception name], [exception reason],
                      [[[exception userInfo] objectForKey:@"backtrace"] description]];
    [resultTextView setString:string];
  }
}
```

The `evaluate` action isn't complicated, now that we know the MacRuby framework API. We start by declaring the variable that will hold the returned object from the Ruby code evaluation. This object is cast as `id`, since we know only that it will be an Objective-C object, not its exact type. We then evaluate the content of the Ruby source text view and store the result into the `object` variable. The description of the object is then set as the text displayed in the result text view. In case something goes bad with our Ruby code, the method is wrapped so it can catch any exception thrown and display it in the result text view.

Fire the app and click the Evaluate button. You should see something similar to Figure 11-7.

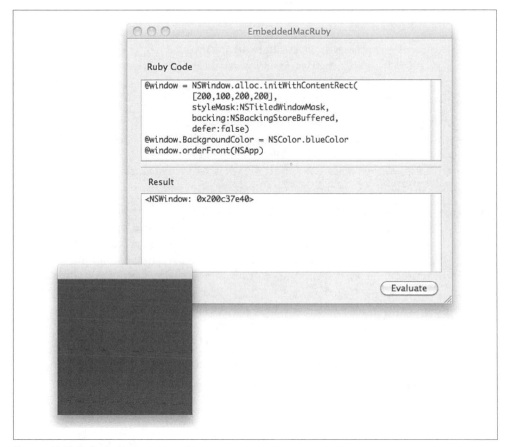

Figure 11-7. Ruby interpreter in action

Creating new objects and modifying them on the fly is really nice, but what about modifying the UI we already created? Well, we are missing a reference to our main window, which we can't access from our evaluated script. To fix that, change the `awakeFromNib` method as shown here:

```
- (void)awakeFromNib
{
  NSFont *niceFont;

  niceFont - [NSFont fontWithName:@"Monaco" size:12.0];
```

```
[rubySourceTextView setFont:niceFont];
[resultTextView setFont:niceFont];

id appHelper = [[MacRuby sharedRuntime] evaluateString:@"module App;\
                def self.setWindow(val); @window=val; end;\
                def self.window; @window; end; end; App"];
[appHelper performRubySelector:@selector(setWindow:)
                            withArguments:window, nil];
[rubySourceTextView setString:@"App.window.title = 'WOOt!'"];
}
```

This time, when the app loads, we evaluate an **App** module helper that we assign to an Objective-C reference. Then we pass the Objective-C window reference to our module so we can access it from our Ruby code. To prove that it works, we add a demo statement that changes the title of the window.

Have fun inspecting your live views and subviews, as well as tweaking them in real time from within your Objective-C app. If you want to find the available methods on the class, evaluate **App.window.methods(true, true).sort** or read the NSWindow Class Reference (*http://developer.apple.com/library/mac/#documentation/Cocoa/Reference/ApplicationKit/Classes/NSWindow_Class/Reference/Reference.html*).

You might have noticed that the Ruby setter in our **App** module is called **setWindow**, not a very Ruby-like setter name. Usually, you will want to use **window=**. However, if we had used that method name, we wouldn't be able to perform our selector. This is because the Objective-C compiler won't accept a selector name containing an equals sign. As a matter of fact, the compiler will reject all selector names containing non-standard characters: =, <, >, ?, [], |, +, -, *, /, `, and more. However, these characters are common in Ruby methods. Thankfully, there is a workaround. You can build the selectors yourself using the Objective-C runtime API, which does not suffer from this limitation.

Here is the **awakeFromNib** method, reimplemented using the **sel_registerName** method:

```
- (void)awakeFromNib
{
  NSFont *niceFont;

  niceFont = [NSFont fontWithName:@"Monaco" size:12.0];
  [rubySourceTextView setFont:niceFont];
  [resultTextView setFont:niceFont];

  id appHelper = [[MacRuby sharedRuntime] evaluateString:@"module App;\
                  def self.window=(val); @window=val; end;\
                  def self.window; @window; end; end; App"];
  [appHelper performRubySelector:sel_registerName("window=:")
                              withArguments:window, nil];
  [rubySourceTextView setString:@"App.window.title = 'WOOt'"];
}
```

We can now perform a selector containing the equals sign.

## CHAPTER 12

Objective-C Code in MacRuby Apps

In the previous chapter, you saw how to embed MacRuby into an Objective-C project. While MacRuby works great for building Cocoa apps, there are some cases where performance and low-level programming is important. In other cases, you may already have a library written in Objective-C and you would like to use it in your MacRuby project.

Dynamic Library

If the Objective-C code you would like to use isn't in a framework, the easiest way to package it to make use of it in MacRuby is to create a Dynamic Library.

Let's pretend we already wrote some awesome Objective-C code that we rely on heavily, and we want to share this code between our projects. Following is the code we are going to try to reuse.

Header file—*Spelling.h*:

```objc
#import <Foundation/Foundation.h>

@interface Spelling : NSObject{
  NSDictionary *table;
}

- (Spelling*) initWithBuiltinTable;
- (NSString*) britishize:(NSString*)string;
@end
```

Implementation file—*Spelling.m*:

```objc
#import "Spelling.h"

@implementation Spelling

- (Spelling*) initWithBuiltinTable {
  self = [super init];
  if ( self ){
    table = [NSDictionary dictionaryWithObjectsAndKeys:
```

```
                @"flat", @"apartment",
                @"row", @"argument",
                @"pram", @"baby carriage",
                @"plaster", @"band-aid",
                @"loo", @"bathroom",
                @"tin", @"can",
                @"mince", @"chopped beef",
                @"biscuit", @"cookie",
                @"maize", @"corn",
                @"nappy", @"diaper",
                @"lift", @"elevator",
                @"rubber", @"eraser",
                @"torch", @"flashlight",
                @"chips", @"fries",
                @"petrol", @"gas",
                @"bloke", @"guy",
                @"motorway", @"highway",
                @"bonnet", @"hood",
                @"jelly", @"jello",
                @"jam", @"jelly",
                @"paraffin", @"kerosene",
                @"solicitor", @"lawyer",
                @"number plate", @"license plate",
                @"queue", @"line",
                @"post", @"mail",
                @"caravan", @"motor home",
                @"cinema", @"movie theater",
                @"silencer", @"muffler",
                @"serviette", @"napkin",
                @"nought", @"nothing",
                @"flyover", @"overpass",
                @"dummy", @"pacifier",
                @"trousers", @"pants",
                @"car park", @"parking lot",
                @"full stop", @"period",
                @"chemist", @"pharmacist",
                @"crisps", @"potato chips",
                @"hire", @"rent",
                @"banger", @"sausage",
                @"pavement", @"sidewalk",
                @"football", @"soccer",
                @"jumper", @"sweater",
                @"bin", @"trash can",
                @"lorry", @"truck",
                @"boot", @"trunk",
                @"holiday", @"vacation",
                @"waistcoat", @"vest",
                @"windscreen", @"windshield",
                 nil ];
    }
    return self;
}

- (NSString*)britishize:(NSString*)string{
    NSString* conversion = [table objectForKey:string];
```

```
    if( conversion ){
      return conversion;
    }else{
      return string;
    };
  }

  @end
```

This code implements a class called Spelling with an instance method called britishize that takes a string and, if a translation is found, returns the British equivalent of the string. Otherwise, the passed string is returned.

This is how we can use our code in an Objective-C project:

```
Spelling* converter = [[Spelling alloc] initWithBuiltinTable];
NSString* result = [converter britishize:@"truck"];
NSLog(@"%@\n", result);
# => 2011-05-30 14:44:09.293 example[73135:903] lorry
```

Obviously, this is just a trivial example to illustrate this concept. For those who don't know Objective-C but are familiar with Ruby, the equivalent code written in Ruby looks more or less like this:

```
module Spelling

  @table = Hash["apartment", "flat",
                "argument", "row",
                "baby carriage", "pram",
                "band-aid", "plaster",
                "bathroom", "loo",
                "can", "tin",
                "chopped beef", "mince",
                "cookie", "biscuit",
                "corn", "maize",
                "diaper", "nappy",
                "elevator", "lift",
                "eraser", "rubber",
                "flashlight", "torch",
                "fries", "chips",
                "gas", "petrol",
                "guy", "bloke, chap",
                "highway", "motorway",
                "hood", "bonnet",
                "jello", "jelly",
                "jelly", "jam",
                "kerosene", "paraffin",
                "lawyer", "solicitor",
                "license plate", "number plate",
                "line", "queue",
                "mail", "post",
                "motor home", "caravan",
                "movie theater", "cinema",
                "muffler", "silencer",
                "napkin", "serviette",
                "nothing", "nought",
```

```
                         "overpass", "flyover",
                         "pacifier", "dummy",
                         "pants", "trousers",
                         "parking lot", "car park",
                         "period", "full stop",
                         "pharmacist", "chemist",
                         "potato chips", "crisps",
                         "rent", "hire",
                         "sausage", "banger",
                         "sidewalk", "pavement",
                         "soccer", "football",
                         "sweater", "jumper",
                         "trash can", "bin",
                         "truck", "lorry",
                         "trunk", "boot",
                         "vacation", "holiday",
                         "vest", "waistcoat",
                         "windshield", "windscreen"]

    def self.britishize(str)
      @table[str] || str
    end

  end
```

To share our Objective-C code, we need to create a Dynamic Library. Create a new
Xcode project and choose the Cocoa Library template in the Framework & Library
category (Figure 12-1).

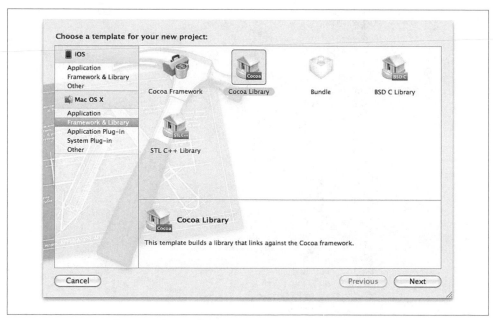

Figure 12-1. Cocoa Library template selection

Call the project *Spelling* and make sure the type value is set to Dynamic. Once the project has generated, we need to make some build settings changes to our main target.

The first change is to the compiler settings so garbage collection is supported (Figure 12-2).

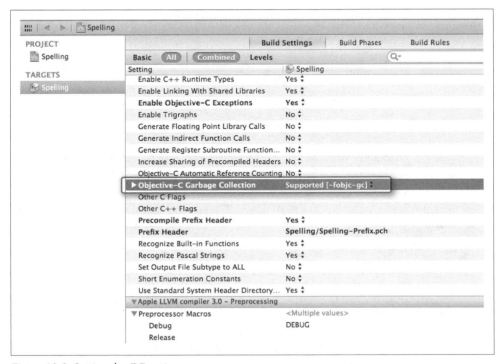

Figure 12-2. Setting the GC options

 I noticed a weird bug in some versions of Xcode, where some compiler settings appear only after I tried to build a project. If you don't see the Code Generation settings, try to build your current project and go back to the Build Settings.

Then we *need* to change a Packaging setting so the Executable Extension is *bundle* instead of *dylib* (Figure 12-3).

Now that our build is ready, we can add the two Objective-C files shown earlier. You can type them or copy them from the book's GitHub repository.

Once you have added the files to the project, we need to do one more thing: add an empty function to *Spelling.m*. Put the following code before the class implementation:

```
void Init_Spelling(void) { }
```

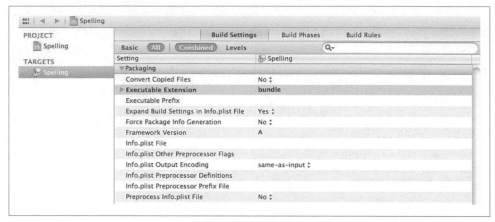

Figure 12-3. Changing the file extension name

We defined a function with a name such as Init_*xxx*, where *xxx* is the name of our Dynamic Library. When requiring our Dynamic Library, MacRuby will automatically call this method. If it doesn't exist, MacRuby will throw an exception. This might be weird, but it's actually related to the way C extensions work in Ruby.

Copy the output file to a new location and try the following from the command line:

```
$ macirb --simple-prompt
>> require 'Spelling'
=> true
>> converter = Spelling.alloc.initWithBuiltinTable
=> #<Spelling:0x2000f8d00>
>> converter.britishize("truck")
=> "lorry"
```

As you can see, the Dynamic Library acts as if it was a Ruby file, and you can use it directly. It's a very convenient way to use Objective-C code in your MacRuby projects.

There are two caveats with using Dynamic Libraries. One is due to MacRuby relying on the GC. All your code needs to be GC-compatible and must be compiled with the appropriate GC flags. The other is that this approach doesn't support BridgeSupport files, so if you use nonobject-oriented items, this approach won't work.

Framework

If you are trying to use a third-party Cocoa library, it will probably be packaged as Cocoa frameworks. Cocoa frameworks are the most common format to share Objective-C code. MacRuby users also should consider using this format if they need to use BridgeSupport (see "Using Objective-C or C Code" on page 149) files. In this section, you'll see what is needed for a framework to be used by MacRuby and how to ship an application with third-party frameworks.

One of the most popular third-party frameworks is called Sparkle, and it is available on GitHub (*http://github.com/andymatuschak/Sparkle*). Sparkle is a software update framework. It's a nice tool that allows you to add built-in update notifications and downloads from within your app. Unfortunately, the App Store policy currently doesn't allow developers to use this framework, because all updates have to go through the App Store. Nonetheless, we are going to use it as an example for this section.

Clone or download the source code and open *Sparkle.xcodeproj* in Xcode. If you look at the Objective-C Garbage Collection section in the build settings, you will see that the GC is marked as supported, so we don't need to change anything. Build the framework and make sure the process goes through properly. At the time of this writing, the current code links against the OS X 10.5 SDK, so you might have to change the base SDK setting.

You can also download the precompiled framework from the Sparkle website (*http://sparkle.andymatuschak.org*).

Once the framework is built, we need to add it to our project. However, we want the application to dynamically link against the framework at runtime. Otherwise, Xcode will link against a hardcoded path when the app is compiled and our application will work only on our own machines or on the machines of users who have the framework in exactly the same path. To do the dynamic linking, we will add the framework to the source files and edit the target to copy it to the Frameworks folder inside the .app.

Now we're ready to build a small MacRuby sample app using Sparkle.

Start Xcode and create a new MacRuby app called MyApp (leave all the template options off). Now drag and drop the Sparkle framework we built earlier into the supporting files folder (Figure 12-4). When asked, make sure you choose *not* to add the file to any targets, but select the option to copy the file. The only point of this step is to give Xcode a reference to the framework.

Now, add a target's build phases by selecting the project name in the Project Navigator, clicking the Build Phases tab, and clicking the Add Build Phase button (Figure 12-5).

Select the Add Copy Files option. A new entry should appear above. Expand the menu, and change the destination to Frameworks. Finally, drag and drop the *Sparkle.framework* file to the area labeled Add files here (Figure 12-6).

To test your setup, you can build the app and look at the .app produced. The easiest way to do that is to expand the Products section in the Project Navigator, right-click MyApp.app, and select show in Finder. To inspect our application structure, in Finder, right-click the file and select Show Package Contents. Expand the *Contents* folder and you should see a *Frameworks* folder containing the Sparkle framework.

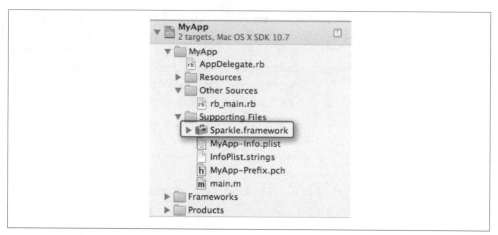

Figure 12-4. The Sparkle framework added to our project

Figure 12-5. Adding a new build phase

The last thing we need to do is load the framework when our code loads. Going back to Xcode, edit the *rb_main.rb* file and add the following line after the Cocoa framework loading line:

```
framework 'Sparkle'
```

The framework is now available in your code and you can make good use of it. You will find a lot of documentation on the author's website, showing how to set your application to use Sparkle.

BridgeSupport

There are some cases where the framework you want to use relies on nonobject-oriented items such as constants, enumerations, structures, and functions. This is the case for the PS3SixAxis framework, available at the PS3SixAxis GitHub site (*http://github.com/mattetti/PS3SixAxis*).

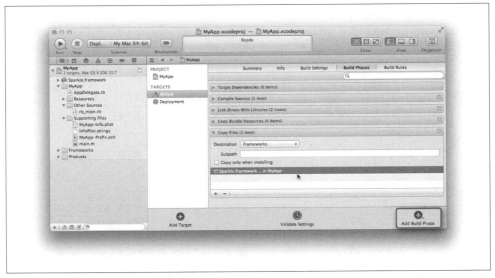

Figure 12-6. Sparkle added to the private frameworks in the copy phase

This framework lets you connect a PS3 controller and interact with it via USB or Bluetooth. Part of the framework is written in C and, because of that, MacRuby can't introspect all the code at runtime. To work around this problem, you or the framework author needs to generate BridgeSupport files and add them to the framework itself.

Generating BridgeSupport is covered in "Using Objective-C or C Code" on page 149, but let's take this framework example to generate new BridgeSupport files.

Start by cloning or downloading the PS3SixAxis repository. I will put the files in ~/ *tmp*, but feel free to put them anywhere you want:

```
$ mkdir -p ~/tmp
$ cd ~/tmp
$ git clone git@github.com:mattetti/PS3SixAxis.git
Cloning into PS3SixAxis...
remote: Counting objects: 85, done.
remote: Compressing objects: 100% (54/54), done.
remote: Total 85 (delta 26), reused 85 (delta 26)
Receiving objects: 100% (85/85), 251.83 KiB | 279 KiB/s, done.
Resolving deltas: 100% (26/26), done.
$ cd PS3SixAxis
$ open PS3_SixAxis.xcodeproj
```

Build the framework and, to make things easy, copy the framework file to *~/tmp*:

```
$ mkdir ~/tmp/PS3Controller.framework/Resources/BridgeSupport/
$ gen_bridge_metadata --64-bit -f ~/tmp/PS3Controller.framework/
-o ~/tmp/PS3Controller.framework/Resources/BridgeSupport/PS3Controller
.bridgesupport
```

The framework is now ready to be consumed by a MacRuby app. As you can see, to generate the BridgeSupport files, we first created a *BridgeSupport* folder inside the *Resources* folder and used the *gen_bridge_metadata* command with the 64-bit and framework flags and stored the output in the newly created folder.

## CHAPTER 13

Using Ruby Third-Party Libraries

In Chapter 12, you saw how to write or include Objective-C libraries in MacRuby apps using frameworks or dynamic libraries. This is very useful for existing Cocoa code or low-level Objective-C wrappers. However, the amount of free open source Ruby libraries is quite impressive. As a matter of fact, there are currently more published Ruby libraries than Perl libraries! This chapter explains how to access these Ruby resources.

RubyGems

Ruby libraries are usually packaged as *gems*, which are library packages used by the RubyGems standard library. A gem includes its own library files, defining a version number and dependencies on other libraries, if any. You can look for gems at the RubyGems site (*http://rubygems.org*). In C Ruby, the default Ruby implementation, use the *gem* command-line tool to install gems on your system. In MacRuby, the *gem* command line is prefixed to avoid conflicting with the C Ruby command. Very much like *irb* is available as *macirb*, *gem* for MacRuby is available as *macgem*.

You can use the *macgem* command-line tool the same way you use *gem*. In this case, I am going to locally install the dispatch gem, a MacRuby-specific gem that adds an abstraction layer on top of the GCD API:

```
$ sudo macgem install dispatch
```

Notice that I'm installing the gem as a superuser (by prefixing the command with sudo), because the gems will be installed in the */Library/Frameworks/MacRuby.framework* folder, which is owned by the *root* account.

While this is very useful, you can't really expect your app users to install MacRuby so they can get access to the *macgem* command line to manually install your app's dependencies. So what we need to do is to embed all the third-party dependencies with our app so nothing is required on the end user's side and all the versions are locked.

There are many different ways to do that, but we will start with the method that is simplest and probably best in most cases.

MacRuby Deploy

MacRuby ships with a command-line tool called *macruby_deploy*, which you can use to prep an application to be deployed to the users. This tool is used in the Xcode MacRuby template targets to compile Ruby source code and embed MacRuby inside an app. But the tool can do much more than that. A quick call to the command shows what it is capable of:

```
$ macruby_deploy --help
Usage: macruby_deploy [options] application-bundle
        --compile                       Compile the bundle source code
        --embed                         Embed MacRuby inside the bundle
        --no-stdlib                     Do not embed the standard library
        --stdlib [LIB]                  Embed only LIB from the standard library
        --gem [GEM]                     Embed GEM and its dependencies
        --bs                            Embed the system BridgeSupport files
        --verbose                       Log all commands to standard out
    -v, --version                       Display the version
```

Because you'll be working in Xcode, you'll normally just modify the Xcode target to change the options passed to the *macruby_deploy* command line.

To illustrate how to embed a gem in a MacRuby app written in Xcode, we'll use a very simple Cocoa app written in Xcode using the Nokogiri gem (*http://nokogiri.org/*). This gem is a C extension (a Ruby gem using a C wrapper), giving a nice Ruby API around libxml. Our app won't do much, but it should be enough for you to understand how to embed a gem.

Start a new Xcode app or download the sample from the book git repository. The only thing this app will do is to parse an XML string and find content inside it. Once the content is found, we will print it to the console. Here is the content of my *AppDelegate.rb* file:

```ruby
require 'rubygems'
require 'nokogiri'

class AppDelegate
  attr_accessor :window
  def applicationDidFinishLaunching(a_notification)
    nokogiri_example
  end

  def nokogiri_example
    xml = "
    <root>
      <shows>
        <show>
          <name>Battlestar Galactica - 2004</name>
            <characters>
            <character species='human'>William Adama</character>
            <character species='human'>Laura Roslin</character>
            <character species='human'>Kara 'Starbuck' Thrace</character>
            <character species='human'>Lee 'Apollo' Adama</character>
```

```
        <character species='human'>Dr. Gaius Baltar</character>
        <character species='cylon'>Number Six</character>
        <character species='cylon'>Number Eight</character>
      </characters>
    </show>
  </shows>
</root>"

# Parse the XML string
xml_obj = Nokogiri::XML(xml)

# find all characters using xpath and extract the node contents in an array
all_characters = xml_obj.xpath("//characters/character").map(&:content)
puts "BSG main characters: #{all_characters}"
# => BSG characters: ["William Adama", "Laura Roslin", "Kara 'Starbuck' Thrace",
# "Lee 'Apollo' Adama", "Dr. Gaius Baltar", "Number Six", "Number Eight"]

# Now do the same but filter the cylons using the species attribute.
cylons = xml_obj.xpath("//characters/character[@species='cylon']").map(&:content)
puts "Cylons: #{cylons}"
# => Cylons: ["Number Six", "Number Eight"]
    end
  end
```

The code is quite simple, particularly if you have used XPath (*http://en.wikipedia.org/ wiki/XPath*) as part of a jQuery application or elsewhere. Look inside the nokogiri_example method. I start by defining a string containing an XML document with some information about the Battlestar Galactica TV show. I then feed that XML document to Nokogiri and assign the returned object to a variable. I use an XPath query, embedding this variable, to find all the character nodes. The xpath method call returns an array that I pass directly to a Ruby map method call, looping through each node and calling the content method. All the character names are now stored in the all_charac ters variable, which I print to the console. I then use another xpath query to filter the characters based on their XML node attributes. Nokogiri offers a really nice CSS3 selector API, in case you are not familiar with XPath.

To work properly, my code obviously needs Nokogiri, and that's why I require Ruby-Gems and Nokogiri at the top of the file.

 Unlike Ruby version 1.9, the current version of MacRuby doesn't automatically load RubyGems for performance reasons. You need to require it manually.

However, unless you installed the Nokogiri gem before, your code won't work. So let's go ahead and install Nokogiri:

```
$ sudo macgem install nokogiri
```

Now you can compile your project. Make sure the normal schedule (not Deployment) is selected and build the project. If everything goes well, you should see the two print statements in the debug window.

Now, click the project name in the Project Navigator and edit the Deployment target to add the extra parameters (Figure 13-1).

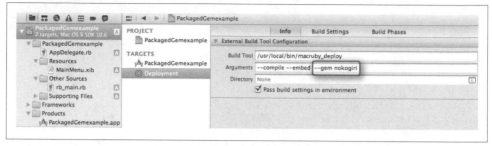

Figure 13-1. macruby_deploy arguments change in the target

 You always have to use the `--embed` option in conjunction with the `--gem` option, otherwise the gem embedding won't work.

Now that the target is properly set, change the scheme to Deployment and build your project. If you look at the package contents (right-click the *.app* file and choose Package Contents) and dig into *PackagedGemexample.app/Contents/Frameworks/MacRuby.framework/Versions/macruby version/usr/lib/ruby/site_ruby/1.9.2*, you will notice a folder called *nokogiri*.

What's also nice with this approach is that you can remove the `require` statement for `rubygems` from your code, making your app's booting time slightly faster.

Finally, if you need to embed multiple gems, you can use the `--gem` option multiple times. Here is an example using the command line:

```
$ macruby_deploy --compile --embed  --gem nokogiri --gem dispatch MyApp.app
```

Index

Symbols

(hash) comment, 17
& (ampersand) passing a block, 173
(GUI), 21–28
+ class method signature, 16
- instance method signature, 16, 126
: (colon) method selector, 10, 56
>> (chevrons) irb prompt, 17
@ instance variables, 194
[], []= MacRuby shortcuts, 46
` (back tick) shell execution, 58
⇒ (fat arrow) irb mode output, 17

A

ABPerson, 153
absoluteString, 49
Accessibility, 160
action, 10, 172
actors, 129
address book example, 167–178
add_contact, 135
add_twitter_friends example, 173, 174
Ahead of Time (AOT) compilation, 162
alloc.init constructor, 12
ampersand (&) passing a block, 173
anonymous methods, 43
API, 191
AppDelegate, 80
Apple Reference Library, 32–35
Application/AppKit Framework, 11, 31, 77
applicationDidFinishLaunching, 8, 14, 84, 171, 186
applicationShouldTerminate, 134
applicationWillFinishLaunching, 84

archiving, 65–69
arrays, 39–41
arrayWithContentsOfFile, 41
art cover, 125–128
assistant editor, 108
asynchronous APIs, 51
attributed strings, 38
attributes, Xcode, 116
availableVoices, 16, 18
awakeFromNib, 200, 201

B

back tick (`) shell execution, 58
beginSheetModalForWindow, 126
Berners-Lee, Tim, 29
bindings, 80, 118–120, 127–132
blocks, 137–139
blocks (anonymous methods), 43
breakpoint navigator, 107
BridgeSupport, 149–152, 210
britishize, 205
bundle, 53
buttons, 9, 23, 124

C

caching, 50
calendars, 44
call, 156
callbacks, 22, 59
CamelCase syntax, 14
cells, 85
center, 88
central panel, reference library, 34
CFDictionary, 41

We'd like to hear your suggestions for improving our indexes. Send email to *index@oreilly.com*.

About the Author

Matt Aimonetti, based in San Diego, California, is a senior research and development engineer at LivingSocial. Prior to joining LivingSocial, Matt worked on video game development at Sony PlayStation; and before that he worked with startups, Fortune 100 companies, and traditional companies. There, he had the opportunity to be involved with captivating projects in different domain spaces from biotech to comics, advertising, social networks, e-learning, and more. Matt joined the MacRuby team in 2008 and was active in the Ruby community for many years prior to that. He developed or contributed to a lot of OSS libraries and frameworks (Merb, Rails, and many more) and spoke at user groups and conferences in the United States and abroad. Matt blogs at *http://merbist.com*.

Colophon

The animal on the cover of *MacRuby: The Definitive Guide* is a northern cardinal (*Cardinalis cardinalis*), a frequent visitor to backyard bird feeders throughout the United States. Although the male of the species—with its vivid, red plumage—is perhaps more easily recognized, the brown coloration of females is also accented in the characteristic red. Ranging from southeastern Canada and the eastern United States to Mexico and northern parts of Central America, the birds favor dense, shrubby areas, such as those found in forests, gardens, and swamps.

Northern cardinals have prominent crests, thick, cone-shaped beaks, and distinctive facial masks, which are colored black in males and grayish-black in females. The birds reach a length of 8 to 9 inches and usually weigh no more than 2 ounces. Their diet consists of weed and sunflower seeds, grains, fruits, and insects, and the birds feed their young insects almost exclusively. While there is a preference for seeds that are easily husked, this nonmigratory species is less selective during the winter months when food is scarce.

Mated pairs often sing together, sometimes as part of a mating ritual in which the female sings and the male brings food in response. If the mating is successful, this behavior may continue throughout the incubation period, with the female singing from the nest. Fiercely territorial, the male seeks out the highest perch from which he can closely monitor for other males or predators. Particularly in the spring and summer, it is not uncommon to see the male attempting to attack mirrored surfaces, mistaking his reflection for a rival.

The cover image is from J. G. Wood's *Animate Creation*. The cover font is Adobe ITC Garamond. The text font is Linotype Birka; the heading font is Adobe Myriad Condensed; and the code font is LucasFont's TheSansMonoCondensed.

Get even more for your money.

Join the O'Reilly Community, and register the O'Reilly books you own. It's free, and you'll get:

- $4.99 ebook upgrade offer
- 40% upgrade offer on O'Reilly print books
- Membership discounts on books and events
- Free lifetime updates to ebooks and videos
- Multiple ebook formats, DRM FREE
- Participation in the O'Reilly community
- Newsletters
- Account management
- 100% Satisfaction Guarantee

Signing up is easy:

1. **Go to: oreilly.com/go/register**
2. **Create an O'Reilly login.**
3. **Provide your address.**
4. **Register your books.**

Note: English-language books only

To order books online:

oreilly.com/store

For questions about products or an order:

orders@oreilly.com

To sign up to get topic-specific email announcements and/or news about upcoming books, conferences, special offers, and new technologies:

elists@oreilly.com

For technical questions about book content:

booktech@oreilly.com

To submit new book proposals to our editors:

proposals@oreilly.com

O'Reilly books are available in multiple DRM-free ebook formats. For more information:

oreilly.com/ebooks

Spreading the knowledge of innovators   oreilly.com

Have it your way.